MA~

Mass interviewing and the
marshalling of ideas to

MARSHALLING OF IDEAS TO IMPROVE PERFORMANCE

The Crawford Slip Method

Gilbert B. Siegel
Ross Clayton

University Press of America, Inc.
Lanham • New York • London

Copyright © 1996 by
University Press of America,® Inc.
4720 Boston Way
Lanham, Maryland 20706

3 Henrietta Street
London, WC2E 8LU England

Library of Congress Cataloging-in-Publication Data

Siegel, Gilbert B.
Mass interviewing and the marshalling of ideas to improve
performance : the Crawford Slip method / Gilbert B. Siegel, Ross
Clayton.
p.   cm.
Includes bibliographical references and index.
1. Group problem solving--Methodology. 2. Brainstorming--
Methodology. 3. Crawford slip method. 4. Group problem solving--
Case studies. I. Clayton, Ross. II. Title.
HD30.29.S55   1995   658.4'036 --dc20   95-43769 CIP

ISBN 0-7618-0165-0 (cloth: alk: ppr.)
ISBN 0-7618-0166-9 (pbk: alk: ppr.)

⊖™The paper used in this publication meets the minimum
requirements of American National Standard for information
Sciences—Permanence of Paper for Printed Library Materials,
ANSI Z39.48—1984

A Tribute to Dr. C.C. Crawford

This book was written to honor Dr. Claude C. Crawford and to foster the use of his invention, the Crawford Slip Method.

We wish to provide the reader some insight into Dr. Crawford as an individual as a prelude to addressing his "Slip Method" for which he is internationally renowned.

Dr. Crawford was born in Texas in 1897 and passed away in September of 1992 in Los Angeles. Characteristically, he died at his desk writing the preface to his final publication, "Authorship for Productivity."

CC, as he was affectionately called, received his B. A. degree from the University of Texas in 1918 and his. M. A. in 1919. He taught Psychology at Carnegie Tech. while pursuing his Ph.D. at the University of Chicago in Educational Psychology. He completed that degree in 1924. He was a Professor of Education at the University of Idaho for three years. In 1926 he joined the faculty of the School of Education at the University of Southern California. He retired from the USC faculty in 1956 and worked as a Management Consultant for a decade before retiring for a few years. In 1973, as he liked to say, he "unretired" and worked actively until his death.

During his tenure at USC, Crawford was the author or co-author of more than 20 books, over 100 articles, and over 100 pamphlets. Crawford began writing using the slip method in 1926 and never stopped. He taught his students the slip method as they prepared their theses and dissertations and has trained numerous others to use his method over the decades.

Dr. Crawford worked out of his "Thinkshop" in the basement of his home. Many groups and individuals around the country sought him out and traveled to Mount Vernon in Los Angeles to learn from him the many insights we try to convey in this book. The Crawford Slip Method is an extremely valuable tool for authors, analysts and managers. We hope we have done justice to this remarkable human being and his distinctive and useful ideas.

Contents

Preface

While Dr. Crawford is no longer with us his "slip method" continues to be an important technique for mobilizing brainpower by providing the means for efficiently collecting and organizing data on problems, procedures, solutions, etc. The method begins with thoughtfully constructed "targets;" slips are then written and subsequently classified and become the basis for reports, manuals, books, etc.

The CSM (as we will sometimes abbreviate Crawford's method) has as its institutional base the USC Productivity Network of individuals who are interested in employing CSM in their research, teaching and consulting activities. The incumbent of the C. C. Crawford Professorship in Productivity Improvement is the intellectual leader of the Productivity Network. (Currently Professor Siegel holds this Professorship which Dr. Crawford endowed).

The extensive bibliography of CSM related publications which appears at the end of this book is indicative of the wide range of applicability the slip method has had over the years. It is hard to conceive of any organization in which one could not find numerous possible applications. The missing ingredient in these organizations is individuals who are knowledgeable of and skillful in using the Crawford Slip Method.

The purpose of this book is to provide for the first time a comprehensive discussion of the method and what it takes to successfully use it. The reader is offered both description and insight into the family of qualitative techniques that are encompassed by the CSM. First we note how data and information are collected and analyzed using the CSM. Then, we illustrate the application of CSM to such generic subject areas as idea gathering, problem identification and analysis, and procedures writing. We subsequently show how the CSM fits into and can be employed with other available methods and techniques. Next, we include illustrative applications of CSM in the form of a variety of case studies which provide concrete demonstrations of what can be produced by using this method. Finally, a recap of significant applications and adaptations of the method is provided in the last chapter. The monograph ends with a bibliography of applications.

A frequent first impression when one first hears of the CSM is that it is a very simple technique that anyone could employ. Don't accept that impression as valid. Once you seriously consider using the CSM, you will quickly come to the opposite conclusion that to use this tool effectively requires a number of skills that have to be honed through careful study and successive experiences.

There are both rational/analytic and intuitive skills involved in the various stages of applying CSM. We are confident that a careful reading of this text will prepare you thoroughly for your use of Crawford's slip method. We wish you well as you begin your process of "acquisition" of a method that will be of considerable benefit to you throughout your career!

Introduction

The challenges that today's leaders face are formidable but not insurmountable. As numerous authors have pointed out, these are chaotic times. Organizational environments are complex and turbulent and their stabilization is an unlikely event in the foreseeable future. Nonetheless we expect our leaders to strive to understand their organizational contexts, to interpret events and facilitate their followers' understanding of and sense of meaning they have of their contexts.

The Crawford Slip Method is a valuable tool for today's leaders. It provides them a versatile technique for fostering organizational learning by identifying problems, capturing ideas, understanding difficulties and deriving possible solutions.

This monograph will provide the reader with a thorough understanding of the CSM, what it is, how to do it and what its unique advantages are.

The basic building block of the CSM is a 2 and 3/4 inch by 4 and 1/4 inch slip which when properly written upon, lends itself to classification and analysis. Use of these slips simultaneously serves a number of important general functions:

- It provides a means for the constructive participation of employees, citizens, peers, etc., and arouses their interest in your endeavor.

- It produces a written record of much tacit or unrecorded knowledge.

- It replaces the typical unregulated flow of ideas from group oral   discussions to one where people talk one at a time with orderly, analyzable input that is being produced simultaneously. (Twenty ideas per person in a 30 minute period).

There are many advantages that are inherent in using the CSM. We list some of the more important ones here at the outset to stimulate you to read further:

- The CSM acquires information from individuals independently; it avoids "group think" and the influence a few individuals may have on a discussion because of their assertiveness, verbosity, etc.

- It provides anonymity which fosters candor with respect to problems and possibilities.

- It is efficient; large numbers of ideas can be expressed rapidly.

- It is relatively simple and inexpensive to use.

- It can produce more comprehensive results than your typical meeting.

- It is versatile; it is suitable for use with a wide array of groups and can be used sequentially with several groups with the resulting slips being aggregated.

- The slips are easy to handle and provide a permanent record.

Some of the important cognitive functions the CSM can assist managers with include:

- The identification and analysis of problems including unsuspected problems.

- The identification and prioritization of possible and often novel solutions.

- The gathering, organization and manipulation of data.

- The performance of needs assessments to plan projects, training, etc.

- The acquisition and organization of information for purposes of authorship of reports and publications.

- The capturing of know-how for purposes of producing materials on procedures and methods improvement, training, etc.

In this monograph we will set forth how to employ the CSM to accomplish the abovementioned functions in the most advantageous manner. We provide the reader with numerous illustrations and case study examples. We are convinced from our experiences that the CSM is an indispensable tool for the effective manager's "tool bag." We are just as convinced that hundreds of other roles will find it to be useful in many of the same ways.

Chapter 1

How to do Mass Interviewing Using the Crawford Slip Method

By mass interviewing is meant the ability to gather the ideas of large numbers of people simultaneously. The larger the group, the better the results! The purposes of data gathering are not constraining. We may be seeking opinions, ideas for improvement of operations, problems and difficulties, or functional information.

The following is the general sequence to be followed in problem/solution identification or just for information gathering:

> targeting
> slip writing
> workshop arrangements
> buzz groups
> classifying slips (Chapter Two)
> iteration for greater depth of ideas

Target Planning

What Are the Questions? Target design is like research design—What are you trying to find out? The answer to this question usually lies in the purpose of the study. The objective is often stated as a problem, albeit not specifically identified. On the other hand, the questions may stem from a research objective. For example, one of the authors was seeking information on mitigation of potential earthquake effects on seaports. One of the research questions was expressed as a target at a conference of experts: What seismic mitigations have been applied in seaports? Additional explanatory sentences elaborated the question to explain that answers might include ideas, programs, investments, and so forth, as well as physical and structural factors.

Often, some sort of need is being addressed and the person sponsoring the research or consulting cannot articulate the exact nature of the problem. It is kind of like what the doctor gets from patients: "I hurt." Your target planning then becomes the equivalent of the doctor's diagnostic process. On the one hand, it may be possible through interviews and dialogue to more narrowly focus the issues. On the other hand, your sponsor may not really understand the problem. It may therefore be advantageous to begin with general targets. This will depend to some extent on the amount of time and the number of iterations of slip writing and classification that you will be able to carry out.

Fishing—a Generic Approach. A typical good beginning is *difficulty* or *problem* analysis. A next logical step is *methods* or *remedies*. Both of these targets are "general fishing expedition" type of questions. They invite slip writers to tick off all the reasons why things don't work, or what ever the question context suggests. Remedies also invite ideas to solve the principal problems that are close to the consciousness of respondents. Interestingly, when we ask for problems we often get solutions, and vice versa for solutions.

Explaining Targets. It is important in targeting that supporting questions and statements be developed beyond the target itself. Supporting questions or statements should stimulate the thinking of slip writers but should not suggest answers. They are discussed in presenting the subject of the target. The idea is to further define and stimulate understanding and the production of ideas. The following are examples of appropriate and inappropriate supporting questions or statements.

Right	*Wrong*
What are the principal problems here at Valley Hospital?	Whats wrong with the administration at Valley Hospital?
—What are the 20% that cause 80% of the difficulties?	—What units are most problematic (Pharmacy, laboratory, patient services, etc.)?
—What have you observed or heard about?	
—What do different groups complain about (patients, volunteers, employees, physicians, etc.)	—What has the Director not been able to solve?
	—Are problems at policy, or operations levels; or personnel problems?

Questions labeled *wrong* obviously suggest topics to slip writers. It is important to stimulate their thinking, but not to bias responses or to supply answers.

The problems and remedies targets will usually be broadest in scope, scope being determined by your charge. Of course even problems and remedies targets can be more or less focused. Thus, it is one thing to ask about problems and remedies for the finance department of a city government. It is quite another to question various constituencies on why the city government doesn't work for them. Depending on the amount of time available for slip writing and the possibilities for follow-on iterations you may want to ask the same questions in different ways. For example, asking *How to's* can bring out ideas not reached by troubles or remedies, yet which are diagnostically equivalent. Or you can ask *what to do*, and then *what not to do*.

Sequencing. Targets should be arranged in sequence so that the *whole* is analyzed before slips are written on the parts of, or special variations on the subject. Feature the overall target title and subtitle as the bull's-eye. Possibly write these on the blackboard or easel paper. Give repetitive reminders of them. This will be clarified under our discussion of slip writing. In any case it is desirable to work from the general to the specific in target planning.

Rehearsal. Your workshop plans in general and targets in particular should be rehearsed. Write a few slips of your own on each of your targets. Doing such a sample of what you will ask others to do may enable you to revise or refine your workshop plans and targets. But your own slip writing is not a sufficient test of how others will understand. A rehearsal with a colleague may alert you to problems you may face with the workshop group.

The following points recapitulate the topic of target planning:

1. Targeting involves development of the basic questions of your research or consulting. As such, targets are directly related to your objectives.
2. Sometimes targets are stated in very general terms in order to identify objectives; for example, what are the problems, and what are suggested solutions in specific contexts.
3. Targets need supporting questions to explain the basic question and to focus the attention of slip writers.
4. Redundancy in targets (some what differently stated), depending on time available, may be helpful in elucidating more information (that is, more slips).
5. Generally, in target development it is best to work from the whole to the parts.

Examples one through four at the end of this chapter illustrate targeting notes.

Slip Writing

Slip Writing Conventions. There are several considerations in formatting slips. These are very "picky" requirements. There are two reasons for the precision. First, individual slips will be manipulated in multiple ways and must, therefore, be self-contained, comprehensible units of information. The second reason for these requirements is that whenever possible the consultant, writer, or transcriber needs to be able to work from the original slips after they have been clustered and configured. Even where the language is changed or several slips are summarized the reader-analyst needs to be able to rapidly track on information in sequenced slips.

First, write only the long (horizontal) way, *not* across ends. Crowd the very top edge (the horizontal edge) of each slip. Slips can then be laid like shingles with only the written part showing. Crowd second and third lines close up under the first one. If you allow a top margin, or if you spread writing downward on your slips, you spoil the shingle effect. Slips are arrayed in this top, down, most recent on top, shingled fashion for two reasons. You do this to be able to review slips you have already written at a glance and to stimulate further thoughts.

Next, write only *one sentence* per slip, never two. If you must explain, do it on a new slip. If slips must be related to each other, clip them together with a paper clip. The continuing slip(s) should have the subject identified. Doubles or triples on one slip defeat the looseleaf principle. Don't number your slips, since they will be rearranged later. Avoid words like *it* or *this*, which lose meaning if separated. Do not use acronyms or jargon unless absolutely necessary. Then, define the terms the first time.

Write legibly and correctly the first time as if they were going to be directly transcribed. Thus, the admonition is to use proper grammar, spelling, capitalization, and punctuation. Write legibly so that a typist can read it. Don't abbreviate words such as "mgt" for "management." Don't use symbols such as "&" for "and."

Feedback. The nature of the audience and commitments to your sponsor will dictate the extent and type of feedback given. A clear understanding of your responsibilities is needed. If you are consulting for management immediate feedback to employees may not be desired. On the other hand, you may be paid an honorarium by the group and both short- and longer-range feed back may be expected. C. C. Crawford himself had several experiences in which he was required to turn around feedback to a conference group over night. Commonly, participants want feedback, particularly if they are interested in the subjects of inquiry. In an intervention by one of the authors at a conference of contract management educators, it was necessary to promise to publish an article in the main journal of the field on the results in order to gain cooperation.

Participants can obtain a general sample of the content of slips, and you can reinforce instructions about slip writing conventions by doing a *"readback."* While they are writing on a second target you might pick out 20 or more slips that are short, legible, and reasonably typical of the whole. You can read these one after the other without comments in a very short time. Doing so gives all a far better cross-section of the group's thought pattern than if you held a half hour's discussion of that target.

Even though it may disturb the shingle pattern of slip writers on the first target, you may want to sample about 10 slips from different individuals in order to monitor adherence to format. In the midst of slip writing you can stop the group and review examples of violations of the rules of slip writing.

One technique, which might be used as a means of providing feedback, has been developed from experience with conducting meetings involving principal speakers. Typically, when the speaker has finished and there are a few minutes remaining for questions, an early recognized hand from the audience results in not a question to the speaker, but rather a mini-speech by the person recognized. As we have all experienced, this often results in little time left for others to ask questions. An alternative would be to have the audience write questions on slips. Either questions at random are selected to be answered by the speaker or perhaps the chair of the meeting selects questions to ask the speaker from slips submitted. We have frequently used this method in training sessions on the Crawford Slip Method in order to conduct a more efficient question and answer session than one in which questions are vocalized by participants.

Short Motivational Talk. Usually, targeting notes are quite explicit on the questions and process of a CSM intervention. This is demonstrated in the examples at the end of this chapter, where even ideas for solicitation of participation are stated. Obtaining the cooperation of participants should begin with a clear statement of the mission of the intervention. There is rarely time for a full-scale sales message, but at least participants should understand that they will be part of a problem solving enterprise, and that their contributions are important. A brief explanation and motivational orientation should communicate this importance.

It is important to communicate that precise, definite, tangible types of slips are needed. People often take pride in being generalists, leaving the details to others. In a workshop slip writers are the "others." While it is true that sometimes some problems can only be stated in general terms, slip writers should be urged to be as specific as possible.

Employees frequently have a great deal to say about delicate organizational issues. However, fear commonly motivates silence. Anonymity can usually be promised because the comments of individuals are combined and eventually synthesized with those of many others. This may alleviate fears and stimulate cooperation. Statements which appeal to the knowledge, experience, and expertise of the audience also may be helpful. Finally, the introductory talk by the leader provides an opportunity to communicate or reiterate the conventions of slip writing described earlier.

The following topics summarize slip writing:
1. There are important slip writing conventions which should be followed if results are to be optimal.
2. Participants desire feedback. Your ability to do this is limited by the situation and the desires of your sponsor.
3. A motivational talk ought to be part of your presentation of the workshop and explanation of the process.

Workshop Arrangements

Slips. First, it is necessary to have an abundant supply of 2 3/4" x 4 1/4" slips. These are cut from white 20 pound bond paper. The means of obtaining a supply of slips from a ream of paper is to have them cut commercially by a print shop—*not to cut them yourself with an office paper cutter.* Slip handling in classification and storage will be important. Uneven sizes of slips that might result from an amateur cutting job will inhibit the process. You may want slips in multiple colors in order to differentiate or control for different respondents from organizational units, levels, roles or physical locations. Your printer or supply unit can cut slips from an 8 1/2" x 11" ream: one cut vertically down the center, and three evenly divided horizontal cuts (see Figure 1). This will yield eight piles of 500 slips or 4,000 slips per ream.

We use special file boxes to store slips before and after classification. These are 11 3/8" x 4 13/16" x 3 1/4" with an inserted smaller box which serves to divide slips and aid in keeping them upright (see Figure 1). These and other support materials may be purchased from the USC Productivity Network Office.

Participant Selection. Ideally, slip writing is carried out in a workshop which is devoted wholly to the objectives of the CSM intervention. Hopefully a second iteration (or even further penetration) is possible with the same or analytically comparable persons. An example of such comparability might be the same function, demography, or organizational level, perhaps differentiated by location or geography.

Sometimes this ideal is not achievable. However, one of the virtues of the CSM methodology is that a "quickie" intervention is possible—not ideal, but possibly better than not gathering slips. This was the type of opportunity seized at the conference of contract management educators previously mentioned. The conference agenda was loaded and only a half hour at the end was available to gather slips on the general subject of learning needs of contract managers. After time devoted to instructing slip writers, attempting to motivate their cooperation, and dealing with logistical problems, there were ten minutes left for the audience to write slips on the two targets of learning needs and suggested ways to optimize this process. Even this ten minute session produced 230 separate learning needs.

Where you can select participants, your objective will be the best guide. Homogeneity or heterogeneity of groups may or may not be desirable. Will you have opportunities for a series of separate sessions, each for a different type of person? Availability of people, or lack of it, may be a major factor in your selecting participants. If you can't get experts, you may have to settle for people within your reach. Often the purpose of the assemblage is mixed. Sometimes we have to give a speech or conduct training in connection with data gathering. When this occurs, the quality of slips written might be enhanced if speeches or training are related to slip writing targets. These and other factors will determine the size of the group. Assuming you have some assistance, size of the audience per se should make no difference in the applicability of the CSM. In fact, assuming that you have help with the logistics of passing out and retrieving slips, more slips—more information is better.

Time Requirements. At least 90 minutes of workshop is desirable to cover several targets. More would be better. Remember, it takes a minimum of a half hour to properly get started with a group newly assembled. Besides introductions and announcements considerable time is needed to explain the CSM and how to do it. If extensive presentations are required relative to subjects it may take half a day before actual slip writing begins.

Logistical Details. The best physical arrangement for a workshop is one in which there is a writing surface for each participant. However, sometimes one is confronted with theater type of seating which does not have retractable writing arms. In this case it is a good idea to have packets of slips prepositioned with a rubber band. In any case, the audience should be supplied with a few paper clips for each group of two or three. These will be useful to clip together a series of related ideas described in more than one slip. Ball point pens should be used by slip writers for clarity and preservation of the data. Pencil-written slips smudge and are often illegible. It doesn't hurt to take along a supply of ball point pens.

Finally, before moving on to the next subject, some further details should be considered. Planning the agenda or schedule is important. Besides the target planning you should plan and write down your tentative time budget. Build into it some flexibility cushions. Your host may fudge on your first half hour and you may not be free to fudge at the end. While some flexibility is needed you should plan on a vigorous and productive pace.

If possible have helpers. Passing out and collecting slips alone can be a major consumer of time, especially in a large group. Hospitality is an important, sometimes nettlesome set of details. Has someone planned for the doughnuts, the parking spaces, the menus, registration, hotel accommodations, name tags and badges? Consult your host on these questions. Pass along insights about complications you foresee. A mere map may help to get people into your meeting on time. What to do about late arrivers? If late comers are likely, think ahead about how to fit them in. They can cause much confusion if they miss the directions. Lastly, conversation by participants can waste valuable slip production time while contaminating independent thinking. Explain the need for writing instead of talking. If people start commenting to each other, stress the need for independent inputs.

This section on workshop arrangements has covered the following subjects:

1. Slips are to be prepared using precise specifications.
2. Selection of participants is ideally driven by your objectives and opportunities for interventions. Opportunistic data gathering may be all that is possible.
3. Time requirements for interventions depend on the state of knowledge for targeting. However, a 90 minute workshop is optimal.
4. The logistics of putting on a workshop involve numerous details. Most important are: the ability of participants to write quality slips and the materials and arrangements that affect this process, the presence of assistance when needed, and attention to detail in planning, including pre-testing of slip writing on targets.

Buzz Groups

What Are They? As you can see from discussion of this method thus far, C. C. Crawford was a very task oriented person. No doubt it is also evident by now that he didn't like free-wheeling methods such as Brainstorming or other techniques based on open discussions. In his opinion the ideas of individuals are often lost. The familiar dynamics of discussion groups are responsible for loss of individual contributions. A person may not be sufficiently aggressive as a discussant, may be intimidated by other members, or may have received subtle queues rejecting ideas, such as through facial expressions and other body language. A common result is withdrawal or, at least, diminished participation.

Dr. Crawford also realized that silent participation alone reaches a point of diminishing return. People simply want to interact. To some extent this is satisfied by breaks after a couple of hours of work. However, one way to capitalize on this need is the "buzz group." The buzz group is a variation on the Nominal Group Technique.

How to Do Them. In the buzz group technique the larger audience is broken up into small groups of three or four persons. The workshop leader should encourage participants to match up with strangers. Individual groups seek a quiet corner or a break-out room. The group should *not* designate a leader or recorder, nor should votes be taken. Going clockwise, each individual, one at a time, without interruption, briefly states his or her best thought on the subject of the workshop. This might be a proposed solution, a clarification, or whatever. After all have had an opportunity to state their idea, the group does a free-for-all discussion of the subject. This goes on for about 15 minutes. Then small groups are called back together in the plenum.

Yet Another Target For Slip Writing. In order to fully benefit from this stimulus activity participants are given another target on which to write slips. Usually this is the last target of the workshop and it is a way of summing up individual ideas and the effects of the thinking of others. The target is merely described as the "Buzz Sum-Up." However, in its supporting explanatory statements, participants are asked to imagine themselves as the sole advisor on the chosen problem. They are to write slips on the actions they recommend. They are urged to give their own views, not a summarization of the thoughts of others. However, it is predicated on the notion that the verbalized ideas of others will interact with one's own thinking to produce new contributions.

Use of buzz groups both enriches the quality of data gathered in workshops and helps to satisfy participants' needs for verbal interaction with others in the process. The following are summary points about buzz groups:

1. The buzz group is a means of introducing interpersonal interaction into the CSM process without disrupting the individually-oriented fundamental nature of the process.
2. Buzz groups preserve important individual contributions before they are subjected to group dynamics which may modify them.
3. Ultimately, the results of individual thinking and group interactions are captured in a final target for slip writing.

Targeting Notes Example One

TRAINING NEEDS OF CONTRACTING PERSONNEL DATA GATHERING AT A CONFERENCE OF CONTRACTS MANAGEMENT EDUCATORS

WHAT TO TEACH TRAINEES HOW TO DO BETTER
MOTIVATIONAL ORIENTATION (Seeking your help)

(1) Curriculum development is a main theme in this meeting.

(2) Two dimensions of curriculum research are: (a) difficulties and (b) methods.

(3) In textbook writing these are: (a) "how to" titles for chapters or sections and (b) advice or directions as to possible paragraph content.

(4) The USC Productivity Network accepted the challenge to help NCMA write such textbooks.

(5) We do it by the Crawford Slip Method of simultaneous interviewing of audiences.

(6) Trainees are of two types: (a) buying for government, and (b) selling to government.

(7) Adverse interests require differences in kinds of instruction (for buying or selling).

(8) Within each type are persons doing many different kinds of tasks or functions.

(9) You each differ in your involvements in these special functions or vantage points.

(10) This means Part I for government and Part II for contractor personnel.

(11) Your inputs can help to identify the chapters for your Part I or Part II.

(12) Your slips are independent and anonymous, and there is one sentence per slip, for classifying.

(13) Please follow some precise directions so slips can assemble well.

DIRECTIONS ABOUT SLIPS (Very important)

(1) Write longways, not across ends

(2) Very top edge of each slip

(3) Only one sentence per slip

(4) To explain, use a new slip

(5) Avoid words like "it" or "this," which refer back

(6) Write out acronyms first time used

(7) Simple words in short sentences

(8) For learners or those outside your specialty

TARGET "A" IN HOW TO LANGUAGE (What to teach trainees how to do better)

(1) Choose between government and contractor's trainees for slips you will write.

(2) Tell what this chosen type should learn how to do better (for buying or selling).

(3) Start each slip with the words "how to," to focus on job activities.

(4) Imagine each slip as a title for a chapter, section, or paragraph (in Part I or II).

(5) Write these in any order, as they come to mind (random order).

(6) Especially focus on functions, activities, or tasks best known to you (your expertise).

(7) Put each on a separate slip.

(8) Remember: Longways, top edge, one sentence per slip, write out acronyms, short, simple.

TARGET "B" METHODS, IN ACTIVE VERB LANGUAGE (Advice, directions, better ways)

(1) Give as much advice as time allows to trainees of the type you chose (for buying or selling)

(2) Start each sentence with an active verb, as in these directions to you

(3) Advise about such "how to" problems as those in Target A

(4) Especially advise about functions, activities, or tasks you know best (your expertise)

(5) Write only one short sentence per slip, starting with an active verb

Targeting Notes Example Two

CRAWFORD SLIP METHOD WORKSHOP: NAVAL WEAPONS CENTER, CHINA LAKE CALIFORNIA

HOW TO GATHER AND SYNTHESIZE DATA, AND DEVELOP ACTION PROCEDURES
MOTIVATIONAL ORIENTATION (Helping you to seek help)

(a) You each have needs for rapid data gathering and analysis from large numbers of individuals representing various organizational units, functions, etc.

(b) This may be part of a consensus building process or it may merely be a consolidation of opinions.

(c) The information gathering may represent problem identification, ideas for implementation of initiatives, or other purposes.

(d) The Crawford Slip Method offers a way of collecting, analyzing, and configuring the thoughts of numerous people rapidly.

(e) If the situation permits, ideas may be gathered anonymously.

(f) Responses are gathered on 2 3/4" x 4 1/4" paper slips.

(g) Distinctions may be made among responses of different audiences interviewed by using different colored slips.

(h) Slips are classified by distributing them into kindred piles, labeling these subdivisions each with a meaningful title, and organizing slips behind each title to facilitate exposition of ideas.

(i) A secondary process utilizes themes identified to develop action procedures for problem solving and implementation of initiatives.

(j) You will be writing slips on subjects, referred to as targets, which should be of use to you in contemporary problem solving as well as learning about the Crawford Slip Method.

(k) Your inputs are LOOSELEAF, one sentence per slip, easy to classify.

(l) As you write slips, keep them in front of you arrayed in shingle fashion, with successive on top of previous ones, but so that all can read from top down.

(m) Please follow some precise directions so your slips fit into the assembly.

DIRECTIONS ABOUT SLIPS *(Very important)*

(a) Write LONG way, not across ends
(b) Very top edge of each slip
(c) Only one sentence per slip
(d) To explain, use a new slip
(e) Avoid words like IT or THIS
(f) Write out ACRONYMS first time
(g) Simple words in short sentences
(h) For those outside your specialty

TARGET A. WHAT ARE THE PROBLEMS OF CONSOLIDATION AND MERGING OF WORK GROUPS UNDER THE TWO MAJOR COMMANDS? (White slips)

(a) Why is consolidation not easily falling into place?
(b) Are there things not being well done?
(c) What has been the position of higher management?
(d) Are there problems of interactions (tasks in which others are involved or have a say)?
(e) Name troubles as they come to mind without regard for any order of presentation.
(f) REMEMBER: Long way, top edge, one sentence per slip, write out acronyms, short, simple.

READ BACK

TARGET B. HOW TO COMMUNICATE THE VALUE OF YOUR WORK UNIT TO HIGHER MANAGEMENT (Blue slips)

(a) What are reasons for lack of recognition?
(b) Are there barriers to communication?
(c) Can you identify reasons why higher management does not appear to value your work unit or, if not your unit, others which suffer from this problem?
(d) What evidence do you have that the unit is not valued?
(e) How can this recognition gap be remedied?

TARGET C. HOW TO DEAL WITH PROBLEMS OF NEED FOR ADDITIONAL RESOURCES OF ALL TYPES, DOWN-SIZING, HIRING FREEZES, AND THREATS OF RIFs (Pink slips)

(a) Are there techniques which you have learned which can help others?
(b) Have you observed attributes of units which seem to avoid these depredations?
(c) Share your ideas with colleagues.
(d) Your ideas will be anonymous.

BUZZ GROUPS
- (a) Now that you have rendered your own thinking on the above targets in the form of slips, it is time for idea sharing and interpersonal stimulation on the topic.
- (b) Form into groups of four or five.
- (c) Seek a corner where noise levels are best.
- (d) Don't name a leader or recorder, nor take any notes.
- (e) Go clock-wise until each person has presented his best idea.
- (f) Allow no cross-talk until each person has presented his best idea.
- (g) Then do a free-for-all discussion in best ways you can.
- (h) Cover the range of topics you previously wrote slips on.

TARGET D. BUZZ SUM-UP: PUTTING IT ALL TOGETHER AS YOUR ADVICE (Green slips)
- (a) Imagine yourself as the SOLE advisor to management of the merging commands.
- (b) Write on slips the action you recommend for solving the targeted problems.
- (c) Write your own views, after comparing yours with those of others.
- (d) Do not try to summarize the thoughts of others.

TARGET E. QUESTIONS ABOUT THE CRAWFORD SLIP METHOD (White slips)
- (a) Now that the method has been introduced, you may have questions.
- (b) Write three questions about the Crawford Slip Method on slips.
- (c) These will be shuffled, and used by questioners who will present them for answers.

TARGET F. CLASSIFYING SLIPS
- (a) Slips from targets A through D are shuffled and distributed among groups of 4 to 5 people.
- (b) Each cluster group will sort the slips into kindred piles based on related subjects.
- (c) As the piles begin to emerge, print a title on a classification card, crowding the top, horizontal edge.
- (d) Three types of classification cards are used to indicate subject subdivisions (see examples).
- (e) Array subject piles in alphabetical order in a matrix layout of a series of columns.
- (f) Once all slips are classified, go back and read each pile to assure yourself that all slips are logically distributed.

(g) Do not be afraid to reallocate slips, to eliminate or consolidate categories.

(h) Under each title, array slips in a logical order such as ideas might be presented in an essay.

(i) Classifying slips in this fashion can provide the basis for direct transcription or dictation of a report.

READ BACK OF CLASSIFIED DATA UNDER TARGETS (As time permits)

(a) Display the complete set of titles developed by each team for each target on flip sheet paper.

(b) Each team should read through slips under each title, avoiding repetition of ideas.

(c) This will be done for Targets A through D, as time permits.

TARGET G. STEP-BY-STEP DIRECTIONS FOR TASKS OR INTERACTIONS

(a) Select a problem or solution identified under the slip writing targets.

(b) Pick one that needs only a few steps in the "recipe."

(c) Restate the problem or solution in its ___ING verb form as a task or interaction.

(d) Underline the task title to distinguish it from slips you will write about.

(e) Write the STEPS in doing the task or interaction, one step per slip.

(f) Place the slips in shingle fashion, the most recent one over the others, but with the top writing exposed.

(g) Start each slip with an ACTIVE VERB, as in these directions to you.

(h) Examples: Verify that this is the meaning of the directive by ___. Or, consult the files on the subject before forming an opinion.

(i) Arrange these slips (like shingles) in best sequence for learners to read and follow.

(j) Don't number slips, since change may be made later.

(k) When satisfied, move the task title slip to cover the slip nearest you (the final step).

(l) Telescope all slips together under the underlined task title slip without reversing sequence.

(m) Even-up corners neatly and apply paper clip from top.

(n) If time allows, do another task or interaction this same way while others are finishing.

(o) PRINT your name, last first, at bottom right of task title slip, as professionally accountable.

TARGET H. MUTUAL AID (Improving first drafts of procedures)

(a) Assemble writers, improvers, and approvers in workshop room.

(b) Work in pairs to improve each other's drafts for correctness, clarity, editorial precision, and readiness to type (except for numbering).

(c) Preserve the shingle sequence throughout, not reversing position of slips as a "page."

(d) Do NOT change the other's slips or sequence without conferring and agreeing (offer new slips for consideration in stead).

(e) Don't number slips for sequence, since changes may be made up to final printing.

(f) First improvers SIGN above first writer after agreeing.

(g) Later improvers sign above previous ones.

(h) Do this with peers, interfacers, persons above, below.

(i) If unable to agree, seek higher jurisdiction or defer.

(j) Submit agreed-on version for adoption, enactment.

(k) Do necessary follow-up technical review and editorial checking later.

READ BACK OF EXAMPLES OF PROCEDURES BY AUTHORS (As time permits)

Targeting Notes Example Three
EPWA MANAGEMENT IMPROVEMENT

HOW TO IMPROVE THE MANAGEMENT, CONTROL AND INTEGRA-
TION OF THE EPWA
MOTIVATIONAL ORIENTATION

(a) You each see the needs from a unique vantage point in the organization.

(b) The composite of all those perceptions can be better than one of them.

(c) Your brains hold a treasure of know-how to get improvement made.

(d) The composite of all that know-how can be a rich resource in many places.

(e) The Crawford Slip Method can build that composite rapidly and productively.

(f) Your inputs are INDEPENDENT, not echoes of anyone.

(g) They are ANONYMOUS and PRIVATE, unseen in your hand writing within your chain of command.

(h) Your inputs are LOOSELEAF, one sentence per slip, easier to classify.

(i) Please follow some precise directions so your slips fit into the assembly.

DIRECTIONS ABOUT SLIPS (Very important)

(a) Write LONG way, not across ends

(b) Very top edge of each slip

(c) Only one sentence per slip

(d) To explain, use a new slip

(e) Avoid words like IT or THIS

(f) Write out ACRONYMS first time

(g) Simple words in short sentences

(h) For those outside your specialty

TARGET A. WHAT IS THE ROLE OF EPWA?

(a) How would you describe the organization's basic mission?

(b) EPWA is a mixture of functions. What over arching general objective(s) will best describe the agency's purposes?

(c) What impact is EPWA supposed to have on its physical and political environments?

(d) Think of concepts which integrate the organizational and functional parts of EPWA.

(e) REMEMBER: Long way, top edge, one sentence per slip, write out acronyms, short, simple.

READ BACK

TARGET B: WHAT IS THE ROLE OF THE EPWA ADMINISTRATOR?
  (a) Are there certain outcomes the administrator should concentrate on?
  (b) Are there areas which should not be of concern to the administrator?
  (c) What should the administrator be doing that he is not now doing?
  (d) If you were the administrator, what would be the activities on which you would focus?

READ BACK

TARGET C: FROM YOUR PERSPECTIVE AS A MANAGER IN EPWA, WHAT ARE YOUR PROBLEMS?
  (a) Are there problems with county central administration and staff agencies (e.g., civil service, CAO)?
  (b) Are there problems of relationships within EPWA?
  (c) Are there problems within your own organization?
  (d) Are individuals the focus of problems?
  (e) Are the problems ones of resources, technology, authority or other dimensions of your organizational life?

READ BACK
BUZZ GROUPS
  (a) Now that you have rendered your own thinking on Targets A through C in the form of slips, it is time for idea sharing and interpersonal stimulation on improving EPWA management.
  (b) Form into groups of three or four.
  (c) Seek a corner where noise levels are best.
  (d) Don't name a leader or recorder, nor take any votes.
  (e) Go clockwise for a one-sentence opener from each person.
  (f) Allow no cross-talk until each person has presented his best idea.
  (g) Then do a free-for-all discussion in best ways you can
  (h) Teach and learn from each other.
  (i) Stick closely to the topics you previously wrote slips on.

BUZZ SUM-UP: Putting it all together as your advice
  (a) Imagine yourself as the SOLE advisor to management on the targets.
  (b) Write on slips the actions you recommend for solving the problems.
  (c) Write your own views, after comparing yours with those of others.
  (d) Do not try to summarize the thoughts of others.

READ BACK

*TARGET D: WHAT BENEFIT WOULD YOU LIKE TO RECEIVE FROM
A MANAGEMENT PLANNING AND CONTROL TRAINING SEMINAR?*

 (a) Recall specific areas in which you feel you need improvement
   and help as a manager.

 (b) Are there areas of your work or your unit's operations on which
   you need ideas and advice?

 (c) What management tasks cause you or subordinates the most
   trouble?

 (d) Are there areas of your responsibility about which you feel you
   could be better informed?

 (e) Are there some areas of knowledge or ability which, if you knew
   them better, would result in improved personal or organizational
   performance?

Targeting Notes Example Four
NEEDS ASSESSMENT FOR LABOR RELATIONS/ MANAGEMENT/SUPERVISORY SKILLS TRAINING FOR A SHIPPING COMPANY

1. DATA GATHERING TARGETS
MOTIVATIONAL ORIENTATION
- (a) You each see needs from a unique vantage point in the organization.
- (b) The composite of all those perceptions can be better than any one of them.
- (c) Your brains hold a treasure of know-how to get improvements made.
- (d) The composite of all that know-how can be a rich resource in many places.
- (e) The Crawford Slip Method can build that composite rapidly and productively.
- (f) Your inputs are INDEPENDENT, not echoes of anyone.
- (g) They are ANONYMOUS and PRIVATE, unseen in your hand writing within your chain of command.
- (h) Your inputs are LOOSELEAF, one sentence per slip, easier to classify.
- (i) Please follow some precise directions so your slips fit into the assembly.

DIRECTIONS ABOUT SLIPS (Very important)
- (a) Write LONG way, not across ends
- (b) Very top edge of each slip
- (c) Only one sentence per slip
- (d) To explain, use a new slip
- (e) Avoid words like IT or THIS
- (f) Write out ACRONYMS first time
- (g) Simple words in short sentences
- (h) For those outside your specialty

TARGET A. WRITE AS MANY SLIPS AS YOU CAN ON MANAGEMENT/ SUPERVISORY TASKS THAT MIGHT CAUSE THE MOST TROUBLE IN THIS KIND OF LABOR RELATIONS CLIMATE. WRITE THEM AS "HOW-TO" STATEMENTS
- (a) Write them even if you know how to handle them.
- (b) Think of them as advice to others.
- (c) Describe the 1 to 5 percent of tasks that cause 90 percent of the problems.

(d) REMEMBER: Long way, top edge, one sentence per slip, write out acronyms, short, simple.

TARGET B. SELECT ONE OF THE "HOW-TO" PROBLEMS ON WHICH YOU HAVE SOME GOOD IDEAS OR STRONG CONVICTIONS
  (a) Write those ideas in answer to "how-to" statements, one sentence per slip.
  (b) These may be step by step prescriptions or general ideas.
  (c) Attach these answer slips behind the problem slip using a paper clip.
  (d) Repeat this process for as many "how-to" questions or statements as time permits.

TARGET C. DESCRIBE MORE GENERAL DIFFICULTIES AND PROBLEMS IN MANAGING, AGAIN, IN THIS KIND OF LABOR RELATIONS CLIMATE
  (a) These may extend beyond direct supervisory relations to the role of, and relations with higher management.
  (b) These might be deficiencies, shortfalls, obstacles, problems, needs, unfinished business or other negatives.
  (c) Do some company policies create difficulties?

TARGET D. WHAT ARE SOME SPECIFIC REMEDIES FOR THESE DIFFICULTIES?
  (a) Give all the possible advice to yourself or anyone else who might do the improving in your unit or outside of it on major reforms or minor details.
  (b) Supply the fruit of your experience or observation.
  (c) Whatever you think worth mentioning.
  (d) Think of it as a giant suggestion box for the good of the whole organization.
  (e) Suggestions and directions for improving the labor relations climate.
TEN MINUTE BREAK

TARGET E. AS A MANAGER/SUPERVISOR, WHAT SPECIFIC KINDS OF TRAINING DO YOU BELIEVE YOU NEED IN ORDER TO DO YOUR JOB EFFECTIVELY?

TARGET F. WHAT KINDS OF TRAINING AND/OR EXPERIENCE DO YOU BELIEVE WOULD HELP PREPARE YOU FOR PROGRESSING IN THIS COMPANY?

BUZZ GROUPS
- (a) Now that you have rendered your own thinking on Targets A through F in the form of slips, it is time for idea sharing and interpersonal stimulation in improving management.
- (b) Form into groups of three or four.
- (c) Seek a corner where noise levels are best.
- (d) Don't name a leader or recorder, nor take any notes.
- (e) Go clock-wise for a one-sentence opener from each person.
- (f) Allow no cross-talk until each person has presented his best idea.
- (g) Then do a free-for-all discussion in best ways you can.
- (h) Teach and learn from each other.
- (i) Stick closely to the topics you previously wrote slips on.

BUZZ SUM-UP, PUTTING IT ALL TOGETHER AS YOUR ADVISE
- (a) Imagine yourself as the SOLE advisor to management on the targets.
- (b) Write on slips your advice to management on how to get the most improvement from all these suggestions (any and all uses, implementations, or follow-ups you can think of).
- (c) Write your own views, after comparing yours with those of others.
- (d) Do not try to summarize the thoughts of others.

2. ANALYSIS, FEEDBACK, AND PRIORITIZATION OF TRAINING NEEDS
- (a) The above data gathering will take place during a half-day session.
- (b) The consultant and the port terminal manager will classify slips during the second half of the first day or the first half of the second day, depending on the schedule.
- (c) Slips will be classified and classification cards written for individual training needs as "how-to" statements/questions under each target.
- (d) A list of training needs will be compiled from all targets, eliminating repetitions under the various targets.
- (e) Individual training needs statements will either be listed on newsprint or typed and xeroxed (preferable).
- (f) In the second session, individual training needs will be discussed with the assembled managers, including a reading of examples from slips classified under the training need statement.

IF TRAINING NEEDS ARE LISTED ON NEWSPRINT:

    (g) Managers will be asked to copy individual training needs on slips, one per slip.

    (h) They will then be asked to prioritize the list of training needs from 1 to N, 1 being the highest/most important need, by writing the number of the priority in the upper left hand corner of each slip.

IF TRAINING NEEDS ARE TYPED AND REPRODUCED AS A LIST:

    (g) Managers will be asked to indicate priority numbers on the lists

Chapter 2

Classifying and Summarizing Slips

Categorizing slips is really the heart of the creative process involved in the CSM. Though you may have differentiated topics in the targeting process, the slips collected are usually an array of linked and unlinked insights. It is by the classifying process that you will establish the topical skeleton and the flow of ideas within that outline. Before discussing the process there are a few points to be made about "nuts and bolts."

Physical Layout and Materials. Assuming that the volume of slips is not great (a few hundred) we use a table top for classifying. You will want to clear a table top area as far as you can reach, and a little more to spare. A smooth, hard surface is better than table cloths which hinder manipulation. You are dealing with light pieces of paper so there should be freedom from drafts or breezes that are likely to disrupt order.

If slips number several hundred or thousands it is best to use a classification tray. These are made from corrugated paper filled with egg crate-type slots which are a little wider than slips and about 3/4" lower. The slips can be visually scanned above the sides of the tray and the dividers. Trays can be made in various sizes. We usually use 60 slot trays, with several of them side-by-side when necessary. The USC Productivity Network Office can supply them in broken down form with assembly and gluing instructions.

Classification and guide cards are shown in figure 1, along with views of the classification tray and the file box. *Classification cards* are used to title and divide categorized slips. Have your printer cut a few hundred cards 3" x 4 1/4" in size from card stock. Exact uniformity of height is a critical factor. Thus, we again admonish you not to hack them out with scissors or an office cutter. It is helpful to have cards in several colors to match colored slips if this seems desirable. Also, you may want to contrast classification cards with white slips. Eventually you may need guide cards for outline levels above the classification card level. These will be described next.

Guide cards Have your printer cut a lesser supply of cards 3 1/8" x 4 1/4" for higher outline levels. The extra 1/8" height lets them be seen above the classification cards when later filed on edge in your slip box. A color contrast with your slips adds greatly to their usefulness. Have your printer cut off a corner from middle of the long (top) edge to the middle of an end. These guide cards can then be used in *right* position for outline level next above classification cards or in *left* position for one level still higher in the outline.

Configuring Ideas Gathered on Slips. First, the analyst needs to read a sample of the slips from each target to get a feeling for variance and content in and among slips. Obviously, one would check to see that all slips face the same way and are right-sided up. Next, shuffle target slips well. This is to break up clusters that come from individual persons. Shuffling will aid in preventing one person's thought structure from influencing your own too much.

Classifying the most general target is now under taken. As stated earlier, this may be a fishing expedition target such as *troubles.* Begin by laying slips face up until kindred piles appear based on commonality of theme. Once you have a few related slips decide on the key word, term, or brief phrase that best represents that pile. Choose key terms as you would in indexing a book alphabetically. Let your first word be the one a person would look under in an index. This alphabetical aid will be important in locating the piles on the table.

An illustration of this process is taken from a situation in which slips from both troubles and remedies targets were classified together. The following are examples of slips which composed the kindred pile:

> Not many people in upper management know much about our jobs
>
> Higher manager needs better understanding of what we go through
>
> Upper management's knowledge is limited to "managing-by-walking-around"
>
> Company higher management is out of step with lower management
>
> Get the manager to live in a world of reality
>
> Upper management argues too much; it causes poor morale
>
> Listen to our problems

Upper management must allow lower management to observe good communication and problem solving
We get new higher bosses every two years who don't know much about what we do
Need to become more aware of superintendent's problems
Upper management needs to do our jobs for a week.

This kindred pile was classified under the title: Knowledge deficiency of the Superintendent's job by higher management.

A note of caution is needed on the selection of classification card titles. It is especially tempting for first-time classifiers to use general categories which seem to both fit one's experience and the data on slips. Accordingly, titles such as "communication problems," "supervision," and "organization problems" appear to be appropriate. Such common topics are usually useless. One needs to title more operationally. For example, the slips in the earlier illustration might have been classified under "communication problems," but so might many other problematic aspects of communication recorded on slips. In classifying you should seek to title at as low a level of abstraction as possible and still be able to summarize related thoughts. Beginning with a very general title usually does not get at the inherent texture or variation in slips.

Write these index words on classification cards. Write ALL IN CAPITALS with a felt tipped pen so you can read them at arm's length. Write the long way. Stay within the 1/4" of the card that will show above the slips when later filed in your slip box. Lay slips on the indexed card so that the index words don't get covered up. To add new slips to the piles, go by the index words, not the last slip you laid down. From the above example, key operative words that should jump out at the classifier will be "knowledge deficiency," "higher management," "superintendent's job."

As you accumulate piles of slips which have been indexed you should begin to array piles alphabetically by the index titles. Lay an "A - -" index card and its piled-on slips at your far left. Lay a "W - -" index card and pile at your far right. Thus, "ACCESS TO SUPERIORS" can be in the "A" position at your far left and "WORKING CONDITIONS" at your far right. Put "ACCESS TO SUPERIORS" near the front edge of your table, "ATTITUDES TOWARD WORK" well up from the edge. If a row gets crowded, move the piles as needed. The alphabet can help you find them.

As we mentioned earlier, when we ask for slips on troubles people often give remedies, and vice versa. Thus, slips from the second target would be classified using the same key words unless new ones are evident, and then a new kindred pile with its separate classification card would be created and placed in alphabetical sequence. In general, both of these fishing expedition topics can be successfully classified under the same titles.

As you go about the categorizing of slips you may find that what began as one category may turn out to be two as it picks up more slips. Some piles you thought were different may combine as you proceed. Just how much combining and expanding of categories is necessary is really based on a combination of factors. First your original motivation in doing the workshop is important. If you are looking for topics which will allow you to penetrate deeper layers of questions, you would want to expand the topics. On the other hand, aggregations of slips may simply not produce all that much variation. Even though a topic has but a few slips it may appear to you as the analyst to be important, and therefore to be recognized categorically. A good rule of thumb in classifying is to be expansive of categories to the greatest extent permitted by the data base, remembering that few slips will use the same words, but many may say essentially the same message. So, the first pass classifying each target's slips will be as expansive as possible of titles. Later, in reassessing slips, or even perhaps as you go, further expansion or consolidations will appear to make sense.

Transition From Alphabetical Indexing to a Structured Outline. How representative are slip writers of the phenomenon you are investigating? If you feel they are reasonably representative, you may want to move to closure on your report, manual, project, or whatever it is. Much depends on the number and quality of slips collected. How adequate is the saturation? How well do you feel that your original felt need can be met if all these ideas are written up for guidance of others? You may decide that you are ready to write it up. Or you may think it best to use these subproblem categories as targets for deeper penetration into more precise and specific know-how.

Whatever the purpose of your intervention, you will be building what will amount to a table of contents. You do this even if you do not believe that it will represent a final product. Perhaps it is only a launching pad for further investigation. The configuration may suggest new lines of inquiry. In any case, you use much the same process you applied in classifying slips, only you are grouping piles of slips behind their classification cards in groups of twos, threes, and so forth. Use paper clips or rubber bands to make each category easy to manipulate as one physical unit. Arrange these banded units in rows according to kinship of content. Perhaps a higher level title is called for to organize several piles. If a book is being outlined, for example, several piles may comprise a section, which when grouped with other clusters will be the basis for a chapter.

Besides kindred relationships (such as subjects of grievances), the grouping process also involves the factor of sequencing of categories (for example, steps in the grievance process, or the logical place of grievances in the labor relations process). Perhaps sequencing is more a question of exposition of ideas. Which parts will your readers need first? How will a proposed sequence affect some of the groupings you had made based on kinship of content? Several designs might be tried. You may need to leave it alone for a while, then come back to it. You might talk it over with a colleague.

Once your outline is stabilized, some of your slips become misfits in their new settings or sequences. Also, you will naturally have made some accidental errors in laying slips on piles. So go through each pile, slip by slip, and correct any misclassifications. You will always have some slips that might go in either of two places. In such cases, place the slip in the pile that is weak rather than in one where the topic is already well covered. One aid in reviewing slips in piles is to arrange the slips in the order that you would sequentially talk or write about them under the classified category. Slips that don't fit should be apparent.

The classifying process is recapitulated as follows:

1. Even when targets are quite focused on narrow topics information obtained from slip writers must be configured to create a logical exposition of ideas. The classifying process does this.

2. A table top or sorting boxes are used for organizing slips into kindred piles by subject matter. Classification cards are used to summarize the essence of these relationships. Guide cards provide the structure for higher levels of classification.

3. Prior to classification for a particular target, slips are randomized to reduce the influence of individual contributors. Slips are then sorted into kindred piles based upon relationships which seem apparent. The nature of a relationship is captured in the title assigned to the pile which is printed on a classification card.

4. Piles of slips should be arrayed alphabetically as they are being classified. Later, in organizing the piles into a structured outline, complete clusters are manipulated as if they were individual slips. The latter are organized into a logical pattern which also takes sequential relationships into consideration.

5. The total organized pattern of slips is reviewed, slip by slip, for proper classification. Slips may be reallocated at this point. Titling language of clusters on classification cards may be changed. Even higher order organization may be modified.

Deeper Idea Penetration

Exploration of ideas in greater depth than that obtained from first round slip gathering is possible. Classification of slips from first round targets often reveals many topics that need to be explored in greater depth. A return to the same group or a group that is similarly attributed (same profession, same organization—different location, same function—different organization, and so forth) are the best audiences for exploration of more penetrating targets. This, of course, is not to say that if your subject demands it, that the audience could not be heterogeneous.

First, classify slips from the initial slip gathering episode and sort them into kindred piles as before. The key point or term for the pile is written on a new slip and is underlined. Key points should be worded as problems or a targets. Sometimes "How to" language is best. The new target(s) then are fed back to a slip writing group. Even if it is the same group that wrote the first batch of slips we have found that statement of sub-problems as targets open up more thinking than did the original targets. This is because slips are really being written on new subjects, and there are more of them than the original targets.

First round slip writing is usually based on a limited number of targets, typically no more than five or six. The classification of first round slips may produce as many as 20 or even more targets. The ninety minute to one-half day workshop is usually about all you can expect to get in participation time. Thus, it might be difficult to cover all targets using the standard method of running a workshop. Instead, the *rotation workshop* is one way of handling a number of topics in a limited time.

In a rotation workshop each of the new targets is assigned a sequential code number. These are pre-stated in targeting notes which all participants should have. Have participants count off for starting numbers, to distribute people equally over starting targets. Each slip written is to be coded with the number of the target by writing it in the lower right hand corner. Have each person write until slowdown on the starting number, then on the next larger one, and so forth. If the last number is reached, the person comes back to number one and continues.

If the group is new to slip writing, or to this specific project, you will need to have all write on number one to establish slip format, coding, and "good habits of thinking" on slips. For each target you should follow the procedure discussed under Target Planning in Chapter One, including some clarifying statements or questions for each target.

This rotation plan can usually yield an enormous amount of very specific and useful content if it is based on a good original diagnostic workshop analysis and sound classification. You should be able to perceive that the group has reached the limits of its knowledge when considerable repetition appears. Targets on which there are few ideas suggest a true limit to what the group can provide. If you were in a position to involve experts on the subject in a workshop, you might obtain greater illumination of the target. If your classification was not sharp, your ambiguous or overlapping sub-targets may cause some frustration and reduced quality. Slips from the rotation workshop should be classified using procedures previously discussed. It should be noted that you will be classifying information at fourth and fifth analytical levels.

In summary, deeper penetration of a subject can be obtained through a rotation workshop.

1. Deeper penetration of subjects is obtained by converting first level categories of slip piles into targets.
2. The nature of the rotation workshop audience will depend on your estimate of who has greater depth of information—perhaps the same or a similar group who participated in the first iteration.
3. Each target is assigned a code number. Participants write slips on successively higher coded targets—moving from one to another as idea repertoires are exhausted.

Writing and Editing

As discussed, the CSM allows us to use the contributions of many slip writers, writing on various targets, to inductively configure ideas under different levels of subheadings which represent successive levels of subject detail. Individual slips with underlined titles, classification cards, and guide cards are used to differentiate these levels and subdivisions. We also discussed "going back to the well" for greater depth of penetration in analysis to build an even better understanding of the phenomenon under study. We now share a few ideas on writing the final output, be it a report, position paper, book, or what ever.

Arranging Slips For Writing. Behind classification cards slips usually have been arrayed as collected. It is important to arrange the slips so that they reveal a coherent set of messages about the title under which they are classified. These ideas may be expressed in no more than a compound sentence, or there may be several ideas in a paragraph, or even several paragraphs. Slips should be arrayed in shingle format, with the most recent idea (slip) laid on top of the predecessor. Thus, you will be reading the shingled slips as if they were a page, from top to bottom. The sequence and flow of ideas, of course, are of basic importance to the exposition.

Editing. We earlier emphasized the need to train and convince slip writers of the importance of writing slips which are fit to print. If you didn't do this the quality of writing in slips you gathered will make you painfully aware of the omission. You must edit slips at this point for all aspects of writing, especially if you plan to directly transcribe the language used. Alternatively, you might read down the shingled slips and either dictate or directly type the copy, modifying language to suit a common style as you go. If you are doing a report, a paper, a research report, or the like, probably recasting slip content in your own words is best. If, however, you are writing procedures, as we will discuss in the next chapter, precision of language on slips themselves is most important.

Uniform Language For Titles. It is helpful to use a uniform approach to wording titles of subdivisions of reports. Three types we use are titles that begin with: "How to?", verbs in ". . .ing" form, and active verbs. "How to alleviate dental patient anxiety about pain and suffering" is an example of the "How to" approach to titling. When used in a targeting mode of slip gathering it easily starts others thinking in action terms instead of factual ones. It is especially useful when slip writers are less educated or sophisticated, and when slip writing time is limited. In writing documents it is a useful format when the learner is the agent in future performance. It is somewhat awkward when another agent must be indicated; for example, "How to instruct your student to alleviate patient anxiety."

The ". . .ing" verb form ("Alleviating patient anxiety _ _ _") is less suitable for use as a targeting format in short-term intervention workshops. However, it is at its best use in reporting, such as recommended changes, and for position papers. It is suitable for expressing tasks and processes that are to be analyzed more deeply, and as titles for check lists of directions for learners or performers. It is preferable when agents in the action must be identified, but equally applicable when the reader is the agent. It is far better than "How to" for major projects to assemble learning content for complex operations.

The active verb form ("Alleviate patient anxiety _ _ _") is definitely the best language for giving directions or advice. It is always directed to the reader of the sentences. It is far better than should do, should be done, must be, is done, or is better to . . . Often it is the response to a task or a process title stated in "How to," or ". . .ing" language. It is of greatest value when best sequence for reading, learning, and performing has been worked out.

To summarize, some helpful writing and editing ideas are as follows.

1. Slips must be arrayed in shingled, top down fashion for transcription, dictation, or writing. They must also be in the order of exposition of ideas.

2. The advantage of slips written in a fit to print format was restated. The alternative of editing while writing or dictating can be done when the writer is in control of the language of content (this may not be possible in procedures writing, discussed later).

3. Three alternative types of uniform language for titles of subdivisions of documents and their relative advantages were discussed: titles that begin with "How to," verbs in ". . .ing form," and active verbs.

Figure 1
Operational Exhibits

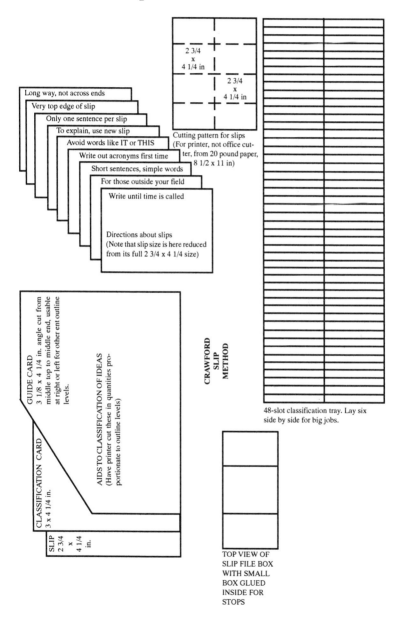

2 3/4
x
4 1/4 in

2 3/4
x
4 1/4 in

Long way, not across ends

Very top edge of slip

Only one sentence per slip

To explain, use new slip

Avoid words like IT or THIS

Write out acronyms first time

Short sentences, simple words

For those outside your field

Write until time is called

Cutting pattern for slips
(For printer, not office cutter, from 20 pound paper,
8 1/2 x 11 in)

Directions about slips
(Note that slip size is here reduced
from its full 2 3/4 x 4 1/4 size)

GUIDE CARD
3 1/8 x 4 1/4 in. angle cut from
middle top to middle end, usable
at right or left for other ent outline
levels.

AIDS TO CLASSIFICATION OF IDEAS
(Have printer cut these in quantities pro-
portionate to outline levels)

CLASSIFICATION CARD
3 x 4 1/4 in.

SLIP
2 3/4
x
4 1/4
in.

CRAWFORD
SLIP
METHOD

48-slot classification tray. Lay six
side by side for big jobs.

TOP VIEW OF
SLIP FILE BOX
WITH SMALL
BOX GLUED
INSIDE FOR
STOPS

Chapter Three

Procedures Writing: When Tasks or Interactions Are the Problems

We move now to a different genre of problem solving. This is about troublesome, but critical tasks or interactions, the solution to which lies in the writing of procedures.

Tasks/Interactions Versus Problems/Solutions

This is different than gathering ideas about important problems or solutions to problems which occur to slip writers. Instead, we are interested in required tasks. Though, it could be the case that the solution to a problem identified through troubles and remedies targets is a procedure. However, problems identified which require an extensive search for alternative solutions are of a different type than those for which the answer is an adequate, agreed upon procedure or procedures. Consider the following examples.

Problem: Cargo handlers do not use safety harnesses.

Extensive search for alternatives, initiatives:
  Analyze ergonomic properties of equipment.
  Search for equipment alternatives.
  Analyze cargo handling work alternatives.
  Survey cargo handlers.

Procedure Writing Subjects:
    Using the safety harness properly.
    Discussing employee performance deficiencies informally.
    Writing suggestions on proposed changes in procedures and
        methods.
    Disciplining employees formally.
Under "extensive search for alternatives" an investigation and analysis may be required, while, under "procedure writing subjects," step-by-step or cookbook-like "recipes" are needed.

Because the procedures for tasks or interactions are more concrete does not mean that they are not important problem solving objects. It is these troublesome tasks that cause otherwise well planned organizational processes to fail. Some tasks may be one-person actions. Some may be complicated interactions in which many persons , disciplines, or jurisdictions share.

Selecting Critical Tasks or Interactions

The authors have shared experiences in writing administrative procedures as managers and analysts. We have come to three conclusions about procedures and procedure manuals as they are traditionally done: it takes considerable resources to develop them in the first place; as soon as they are developed they tend to be out of date; and when they are updated it is usually not concurrent with changes in work processes. The strategy of development for most manuals is to cover all or most procedures. This usually exacerbates the three problems.

Dr. Crawford's strategy for procedures development was two-fold. First, the Pareto Optimum is the criterion applied in selecting troublesome tasks for procedures writing. This is the famous hypothesis that 20 percent of the tasks cause 80 percent of the error or confusion. Thus, it is reasoned that by control of these trouble makers organizational productivity will be vastly improved. The second Crawford strategy for procedures development is that both selection of candidate tasks and the writing of step-by-step procedures is done by the people who do the work. In other words, the people who live with the daily consequences of the problems should devise the best way to standardize action. Co-workers and supervisors assist in this process by reviewing proposed procedures. Alternative steps or sequencing, or choice of words may be suggested. The proper statement is negotiated until all proximate parties agree on it. The optimum contribution is achieved when all (or at least a representation of) persons in the process participate, including supervisors, and perhaps extending across departmental lines to include knowledgeable employees in the chain of processing.

Time and Representation of Participants

Your ability to structure representation in the workshop in particular and available time of participants in general are important. If possible, there should be representatives of relevant organizational functions, locations, levels, or however critical variance might occur for procedures. If you are able to assemble individuals who are related through participation in common processes you are in a unique position to improve organizational productivity. The amount of time available for individual participation is another critical factor. Time and representation can be trade-offs.

A good example of the time-functional representation trade-off was an intervention by Dr. Crawford with the Tactical Air Command in developing a procedures manual for the contracting function. Ninety people from around the nation and the world were assembled. Participants ranged from sergeants to colonels, and equivalent civilians. They were pre-selected to represent all bases in the Tactical Air Command and the headquarters, plus a balanced representation of the different kinds of contracting functions. Additionally, there were about ten representatives from other Air Force commands. Three mornings were available in which to write and agree on procedures for the contracting function throughout the command. Proof that the result was well done lies in the fact that other commands adopted and reprinted the 100-page manual developed for use in their own contracting.

The ninety persons had been pre-selected for the conference, to cover all the specialties and Air Force bases in representative ways. The key target was to choose tasks on which each one's successor would need help. This provided a good prospect of covering the whole range of tasks well. Thus, each participant choose a task for the first procedure draft by two criteria: a) troublesome to a successor; and b) well known to the writer. Crawford expected and received more than one set of procedures for each of a few tasks by the end of the second morning. Duplications were cleared out by the third morning by groups with common tasks selecting the best, or merging good features in some cases. It was expected that there would be some gaps as well as duplications.

Writing First Drafts of Procedures

As with other aspects of the CSM, there are some specific requirements to follow in writing drafts of procedures to make the process efficient. The following directions are discussed and placed in the hands of procedure writers as targeting notes:

> *Writing first drafts of procedures*
> Write task title in —ing form on task title slip.

Underline task title slip to distinguish it from slips
　　written about it later.
Lay it face up before you to start "shingles."
Write steps for doing task, one per slip, *not* numbered.
Word each simply, for learners to understand.
Arrange like shingles, overlapping blank areas.
Check for correctness, clarity, sequence.
Move task title slip from top of shingles to bottom.
Telescope together and even up corners exactly.
Apply a paper clip from *top* of cluster.
Print your name, last first, at bottom right of task
　　title slip, as the accountable person.

As you can see, following these instructions will have the effect of standardizing language and typographical format so as to be assembled without rewriting, and facilitating manipulation of the slips as changes are made in content or sequence.

The face-up shingle arrangement on the table will provide writers and improvers (below) the ability to scan sequences. Slips should not be numbered for sequence because improvers may suggest alternative ordering. Numbering or other sequence designation is left to very last editing and proof reading stages.

Refinement and Improvement of Procedures

Usually the same workshop people who do the diagnostic analysis, identify the troublesome tasks, and write the first drafts also do the checking, improving and adopting. The targeting instructions for improving procedures are as follows:

Improving and adopting procedures
Assemble procedure writers, improvers, adopters in one
　　workshop.
Work in pairs to check drafts for correctness,
　　completeness, sequence, clarity, fitness to print.
Preserve shingle sequence throughout, not reversing it.
Don't number slips, since sequence may change.
Don't change another's slips until you both agree.
First improver *sign* above first writer after agreeing.
Later improvers sign above previous ones.
Do this with peers, interfacers, persons above, below.
If unable to agree, seek higher jurisdiction or defer.
Submit agreed-on version for adoption.
Do necessary follow-up technical review and editorial
　　checking later.

Who does one ask for criticism? Availability is a pretty good criterion since all persons will have been assembled because of some awareness or expertise. Note that improvers do not make direct changes without agreement of the writer. Sometimes there is fundamental disagreement between original procedure writers and subsequent improvers. In these cases it is good to write two (or more) sets of procedures to be drafted and signed by those who advocate them. Options can be offered to a decision maker.

Procedures writing as a problem solving strategy is summarized as follows:

1. Procedures writing is a problem solving strategy that works where step-by-step procedures can overcome the difficulty. In being developed, the steps are agreed upon by knowledgeable persons, such as those related in flow processing and by supervisors.

2. Tasks or problems for which procedures writing is the solution are *critical* ones—characterized by the Pareto Optimum criterion. This avoids the trap of writing procedures for everything.

3. People who do the work write the procedures, and others in the flow, or otherwise familiar with the task, participate by criticizing and approving.

4. Procedures are written as steps, one per slip. They are arranged in shingle fashion to read them as a page. Improvers negotiate content, language, and sequence of the process for completing the task.

At this juncture, the reader should have a good idea about the use of the Crawford Slip Method, and its variations, as information gathering and problem solving techniques. In Chapter four we will discuss several well known methodologies and frameworks in which the CSM can be a useful adjunct tool in data gathering and analysis.

Chapter Four

The CSM as a Supporting Technique for Other Methods

Primarily because of its information gathering and analysis utilities, the CSM is useful as a supporting technique for various methodologies. A sample of such techniques include: Nominal Group Technique, Delphi Technique, scenario writing, library and documentary research, interviewing, creative thinking, on-the-job-training and learning (OJT/OJL), job analysis, organization development and related change intervention technologies, training needs assessment, computer requirements analysis, and Total Quality Management (TQM).

Nominal Group Technique

This method is used with discussion groups when it is desired that interpersonal dynamics be minimized in order to facilitate individual expression of ideas. It is the same technique used for "buzz groups" which was previously discussed as a way of capitalizing on the natural tendency of participants to want to verbalize ideas which emerged during slip writing on targets. However, it facilitates expression of everyone's best thinking while minimizing perceived inhibitions which originate in the group. Thus, we have considered the Nominal Group Technique to be a supplement to the CSM. Alternatively, the CSM might be used to supplement the nominal group process by asking participants to write slips on topics which seem pertinent, just before the break up of groups. Where multiple groups are used, the CSM may provide comprehensive insights for the conference/workshop as a whole.

Modified Delphi

The Delphi Technique employs experts who are asked to give anonymous opinions on future outcomes or events. Usually a series of rounds of questionnaires is sent to individual experts without physically assembling them. After each round the results are analyzed for consensus and a feedback report is developed, generally as the median and quartile rankings, on which individuals may identify themselves relative to group thinking. In subsequent rounds outlyers on predictions are asked to reconsider and justify their positions. These data, in turn, are fed back to participants. The number of rounds is limited by the extent to which leading questions and issues appear to have been answered and by the willingness of experts to continue to participate.

A CSM adaptation of the Delphi Technique might involve CSM interventions at conferences lasting more than one day or which reconvene intermittently. The use of slips would maintain the anonymous nature of the process. Slip writers would write slips on the research question(s). These would be clipped together for individuals and later classified by the process managers who would develop a feedback report in the delphi manner. Usually, overnight turn around of classified slips and the feedback report is possible, and therefore multiple rounds may be pursued.

Scenario Writing

Scenarios are conceptualizations of trends and their interrelationships into written descriptions of possible future states. In using the CSM approach to scenario writing anonymity presumably would not be a problem. Therefore, a variation on the procedures writing approach used in CSM is appropriate.

A first slip writing target might be to describe alternative futures to be studied and their time period of occurrence or, alternatively, futures and time period could be givens. Next, once alternatives and the time period are selected, factors or events are described which may have impacts and cross-impacts on directions of emerging futures. Then, word pictures are written that describe significantly different futures that may result from interplay of the variables under study. Of course, these are written one idea per slip, the totality of which for each future are arrayed in shingle fashion under a title slip (underlined) for each future.

Other participants would then review word pictures for the different futures written by an individual. Changes would be negotiated and both would sign the title slip. This process would be repeated by other improvers who review the draft scenarios until agreement or several alternatives result.

Library and Documentary Research, Interviewing, and Creative Thinking

For archival research the CSM is used to take notes, to develop bibliography, and to organize notes for manuscript writing. Notes are taken from a source, one sentence per slip. When several sentences are required to record an idea, concept, or quote, the several slips are clipped or banded together. The author and source pages of notes and quotes are indicated at the bottom of the top slip. A bibliographical slip is prepared for each source and temporarily filed at the front of all slips from that source. Eventually, all clusters of slips from all sources are classified as if they were individual slips under various subject headings in sequence of the flow of ideas for the manuscript. When slip clusters are so classified bibliography slips are separately organized to be used for notes and references.

Interview notes are handled similarly except that there are no source slips. An exception to this may be where interviews are conducted with several sources. In this case, source slips would be treated the same as in archival research. Use of Crawford slips for interview note taking is easiest when the slips are padded. At the time you are having a printer cut up slips have a supply of them padded. This way, continuity of idea flow in the interview can be maintained without worrying about slip handling problems. To the extent possible, one idea in no more than one compound sentence per slip is recorded, and the rest of the slip writing conventions are followed. Eventually, slips are detached from pads and classified as they are in other slip writing interventions.

Creative thinking mechanically follows the same procedures as are involved in slip writing for targets in a workshop. The difference is that you individually will put down ideas on a subject, one sentence per slip, multiple slips on the same thought clipped together. As in the case of gathering slips from several participants, ordering of ideas is not important as you write. Rather, harvesting them as quickly as they occur to you is the primary concern. Ideas will be organized later in the classification process. If sequence of thoughts is important follow instructions for procedure writing.

On the Job Training and Learning (OJT/OJL)

OJT/OJL is basically an application of procedures writing. Information on most troublesome tasks in work processes must first be determined. Procedures should then be written by experts in the process—

experienced employees and supervisors. This process is particularly useful in situations in which technological changes occur frequently, and especially where the educational limitations of the work force necessitate this form of functional education. For example, in the armed forces, a combination of new technology and inadequate educational preparation of persons who are to use equipment almost makes it mandatory to develop instructions understandable with a sixth grade level of reading comprehension. Further, through a training of trainers process many supervisors can be taught to utilize the CSM in future situations such as development of technical manuals and manual supplements.

Job Analysis

While there are many job analysis methodologies, some serving quite specific purposes, most seek information from which inferences about human performance attributes may be derived. In human resources management, information on the work to be performed and the knowledge, skills, abilities, and personal attributes (KSAPs) needed for performance are sought through job analysis. The CSM can be particularly useful for both the identification of tasks and KSAPs.

Experts (supervisors and experienced workers) are group interviewed usually in a series of rounds. The first round seeks information on tasks or functions of the job. Subsequent rounds seek rankings of tasks in terms of importance, time, and criticality; ultimately inferences about KSAPs needed for acceptable performance of tasks or functions are sought. Applications of the CSM in efficiently gathering and ranking task and KSAP information should be obvious.

Other Group Interviewing Applications

Various organizational change interventions, such as OD, may be assisted in information gathering phases by using the CSM as a mass interviewing, data organizing, and feedback technique. Training needs may be assessed as an outcome of job analysis as previously described. The CSM is also useful for mass interviewing persons to determine work related problems from which training needs are stated and/or inferred. Finally, in developing computer requirements usually it is necessary to engage system users in a series of rounds to determine functions, data requirements, output formats, hardware and software needs, and other information. The CSM can be useful for gathering and integration of information systemically and organizationally.

Total Quality Management

Fully describing the process and values of TQM is beyond the scope of this discussion. However, under a TQM environment emphasis is on the continuous improvement of processes which produce organizational outputs. Functional departmentation which may intersect processes is deemphasized in favor of perfecting lateral flows. Employees are empowered to improve the segments of the processes in which they work through team interventions. Employees are trained in various work improvement and control technologies. They are also supported by technical specialists. Techniques used by employees include: flow charting, Pareto analysis, statistical quality control, survey research, cause/effect analysis, and other technology.

CSM procedures writing is a version of flow charting, and can be helpful in describing as well as improving systems. Further, since employees are continuously immersed in system improvement and problem solving, the CSM is useful in problem identification. This is done as it has been described earlier or in connection with data gathering for cause/effect analysis using the fishbone pattern.

Chapter 5

Case One:
The Century Freeway Project

Importance of This Study
   This study is an example of use of the CSM as part of a larger information gathering intervention in a consulting assignment. It highlights the
processes of target development, decision making about organizing data
gathering workshops, and ultimately the classification of data from these
interventions. The substance of the study tells us a great deal about the
difficulties of achieving economic development of a population sector.

Background
   When construction began on the Century Freeway in Los Angeles in
the Spring of 1982, hopes were high that this, the then most expensive
freeway ever built in the United States, would point the way toward a
more enlightened era of urban road building.
   Instead of ripping through neighborhoods of poor people, scattering
inhabitants to the four winds, the freeway would be built with care and
with a conscience. Construction was to be with the participation of racial
minorities and women and by residents of low-income communities that
lie along the freeway route, including Compton, Lynwood, Watts, and
Willowbrook.
   These details were spelled out in a 1981 federal court consent decree
that ended a decade of litigation and was signed by the California Depart-

ment of Transportation, which would build the project, the Federal Highway Administration, which would provide 92 percent of the money, and the Center For Law in the Public Interest, representing a coalition of plaintiffs who had sued to block the freeway in 1972.

However, by 1987, as the project was implemented, various aspects of the plan unraveled: construction was on schedule but cost was very high; construction costs for housing were extraordinary and vacancy rates were high; minority employment goals, except for females, were met; attempts at utilizing minority and female-owned contractors had failed (many had gone broke and/or dropped out of the program); and the expected economic boom for the corridor cities had failed to materialize.

Underlying the failure was the lack of an effective mechanism to enforce the agreement. The *Los Angeles Times* suggested that the trouble began with selection of the Department of Housing and Community Development, a then small and unknown state agency, to run the program (December 27, 1987: 75). Particularly distressed with the housing failures, the Center for Law in the Public Interest moved to transfer program responsibility from the state to a new public-private partnership to build remaining units.

The court had set up two organizations to carry out the intent of the consent decree: the Century Freeway Affirmative Action Committee (CFAAC) to monitor minority and women employment, and the Century Freeway Technical Assistance Project (CFTAP) to help small minority and female firms function effectively as subcontractors. Judge Pregerson first handled the Century Freeway litigation as a federal district judge, but retained the case when he moved to the U.S. Ninth Circuit Court of Appeals in 1979. His perception was that: "This is not a case where one side wins and the other side loses. You don't have that here. Its an ongoing relationship, in which everybody wins if the project is completed according to the provisions of the consent decree (*Los Angeles Times*, December 27, 1987: 78)." However, delays and under achievement of consent decree requirements resulted in the ordering of management studies by Judge Pregerson in March of 1988. Two consulting firms were selected, Price Waterhouse to study problems of women and minority business enterprise (W/MBEs) , and another firm to review and evaluate obstacles to employment of minorities and women. RJA was selected as a subcontractor of Price Waterhouse. The writer worked with the RJA group.

Targets and Workshop Groups

The Price Waterhouse staff initially researched background information on the case. Important sources were the litigation record, a series of articles by the *Los Angeles Times* on the freeway and its problems, and some initial interviews. Various documents were identified as being in the files of major actors in the case such as: the California Department of Transportation (Caltrans), the Century Freeway Affirmative Action Committee (CFAAC), the Century Freeway Technical Assistance Project (CFTAP), the Center For Law in the Public Interest, various corridor cities, major and minor contracting firms, and financial institutions and sureties. The idea of using the Crawford Slip Method had been introduced by RJA early on as a way of mass interviewing the various constituencies in the case.

From the preliminary analysis a series of research questions were developed.

Financial Problems of W/MBSs:

1.   What are objective criteria of financial success and failure for Century Freeway W/MBEs? How are success and failure measured?
2.   Among Century Freeway W/MBEs, how many have been financially successful, and how many have been financially unsuccessful (bankruptcies, withdrawal from Century Freeway bidding)?
3.   What are the characteristics of successful small businesses? Where do the W/MBEs fall short of these?
4.   What have been the causes of success and failure?
5.   What "financial assistance" is necessary for W/MBEs, and how should it be developed?
6.   What steps should be taken to ensure (monitor) greater successful experience among W/MBEs?

Dispute Resolution Between Primary Contractors (Primes) and Subcontractors (Subs):

1.   What is the magnitude (incidents, dollar value) of disputes between primes and subs (W/MBEs) to date (for freeway projects, for housing projects)?
2.   What is the nature of, and what are the causes of prime/sub disputes? What types of disputes cause the most problems? What 20 percent of the disputes cause 80 percent of the problems?
3.   What are the present means for resolving prime/sub disputes? Are these processes effective? (Freeway projects, housing projects)
4.   What structure or process changes are necessary to more fairly and successfully resolve prime/sub disputes?

Subcontractor Substitution:

    1.   What is the magnitude (incidents, dollar value) of W/MBE substitution?

    2.   What are the major causes of subcontractor substitutions?

    3.   How should structure or processes be changed to (1) permit proper, "good faith" substitutions of W/MBEs to occur and (2) prevent improper or intentional substitutions of W/MBEs to occur?

Technical and Management Assistance:

    1.   What is the nature and extent of technical and management assistance provided to W/MEs to date?

    2.   What technical and management assistance should CFTAP not be expected to provide?

    3.   Is CFTAP managed effectively and cost efficiently (within the terms of the contract)?

    4.   What steps should be taken to ensure that CFTAP is providing the necessary services to W/MBEs in a timely, effective and efficient manner?

Various group and individual interviewees were then identified. Initially, groups identified for Crawford Slip sessions were:

    The Freeway Group: major prime contractors, Caltrans, the Federal Highway Administration, Los Angeles County Transportation Commission;

    The Housing Group: Corridor Cities, small and large contractors, corridor cities, the Department of Housing and Community Development.

    Financial Institutions and Sureties: lenders, bonding agencies.

    CFAAC Board of Directors.

    Corridor Cities: planners, building officials, elected and administrative officials.

Financial institutions and sureties were later designated to be covered by individual interviews because of the smallness of the group.

The nine members of the CFAAC Board of Directors and the other four groups participated in CSM sessions conducted, one and half hours each, on one day, with a break for a luncheon. The general topic of the CSM workshops was: How to achieve the multiple objectives of the Century Freeway Project?"

Based on the preliminary research questions outlined above several slip writing targets were developed. Targets used for different groups were the following:

	Groups			
Target	*Fwy Gp*	*Hsg Gp*	*CFAAC Bd*	*Cities*
What are the financial problems of women and minority business enterprises (W/MBEs)?	X	X		
What is the role of CFTAP in technical, management, and financial assistance provided to W/MBEs?	X	X		
What are the main causes of substitution of women or minority subcontractors by primes on the freeway/ housing projects? Use examples to illustrate the causes of subcontractor substitution.	X	X		
What are the existing mechanisms or approaches for resolution of disputes, other than subcontractor substitution, between primes and subs on the freeway projects?	X	X		
What are/should be the roles of CFAAC Board and staff, and Caltrans in certification, and subcontractor substitution, and other areas of disputes?			X	
What is the performance quality of the CFAAC staff?			X	
What is the ability of the CFAAC Board and staff to perform?			X	
What are the ways of improving relationships between CFAAC and CFTAP?			X	

| *Target* | Groups | | | |
	Fwy Gp	*Hsg Gp*	*CFAAC Bd*	*Cities*
What problems has or will the Century Freeway Project create for your jurisdiction?				X
Why have women and minority business enterprises experienced difficulties in working on Century Freeway projects?	X			
What have been the problems your jurisdiction has experienced in using and supporting W/MBEs on public works construction and housing projects?				X
What solutions to these problems of using W/MBEs on public works, construction, and housing projects has your jurisdiction devised and applied?		X		
Buzz groups on best thinking.	X	X	X	X
Buzz sum-up; advice to Judge Pregerson.	X	X	X	X

Constraints and Modifications

Other than decisions that were made early on concerning where the CSM would be applied versus use of other data gathering techniques, no constraints were placed on the CSM. Also, no modifications to the methodology were required.

In deciding on the logistics of data gathering a decision was made to hold workshops for homogeneous groups, such as all corridor jurisdiction representatives, rather than having mixed groups. If the latter mode were selected differentiation of group representation would have been achieved by using different colored slips. Mixed groups were considered initially, but it was found that it was easier to obtain related groups at the same time.

Findings/Outcomes

CSM findings were merged into consulting report conclusions and recommendations inasmuch as the method was used primarily as one among several data gathering techniques. However, an example of a partial report from classification of slips for one of the four groups, the Freeway Group, illustrating one major subtitle, is shown in the Appendix to this chapter. The report shows the pattern of slip classification under major and minor titles. It also illustrates results of the process of arraying slips in shingle fashion under subtitles, then proceding to write a narrative.

The upshot of this analysis and the larger study of which it was a part was the opening of the Century Freeway to automotive traffic in 1993. The extent to which W/MBEs increased their effective participation in the project between 1988, when the court ordered study was undertaken, and 1993 when the Freeway was opened, is not known. It is knowable. That is, this information could be researched, but it is beyond the scope of this exposition to do that.

APPENDIX
CENTURY FREEWAY MANAGEMENT STUDY
ANALYSIS OF SLIPS FROM ONE MASS INTERVIEW GROUP

The Freeway Group

The workshop was held for freeway related organizational representatives, consisting of 26 persons, at the Airport Park Hotel, Inglewood, California, June 29, 1988.

A. Financial Problems of Women and Minority Business Enterprises (W/MBEs)

1. *Lack of capital or collateral.* These factors have inhibited W/MBEs in various ways, including the extremes of inability to initiate a contract or to bid, on the one hand, to bankruptcy, on the other. Lack of working capital is one of the greatest problems; in combination with poor cash flow, W/MBEs cannot absorb cost overruns which are inherent in construction. The combination of lack of collateral, lack of assets extant, and lack of experience with larger jobs inhibit contractors from obtaining bonds and loans. As a consequence, W/MBEs rarely reach the point of becoming profitable businesses. To make matters worse, W/MBEs frequently have been unaware of requirements for operating capital. For example, payrolls may double before the sub receives the first progress payment.

2. *Bonding and insurance.* Both bonding and insurance are difficult for W/MBEs to obtain. Bonding is generally a problem until the contractor establishes a successful "track record." One person suggested that Caltrans and the court should provide bonds for W/MBEs, or see that they can successfully bid on contracts. Insurance is also difficult for W/MBEs to obtain at affordable rates. In the opinion of one person, W/MBEs who cannot be bonded should not be permitted to bid. This person feels that W/MBEs have been mislead about how easy it is to become a successful contractor.

3. *Payments.* Prime contractors have been known to delay payments to subs after they, themselves have been paid. Not uncommonly, this results in subs being forced out of business. Reasons for this payment delay vary, but at times it is to bolster the cash position of the prime. This problem occurs in spite of the fact that Caltrans has reasonable payment provisions for general contractors; however, subs are at the mercy of these primes. At best though, Caltrans is always in arrears in progress payments; there is not "up front" money for initial operations. This situation is exacerbated by W/MBE ineptitude in completing paper work to get paid.

4. *Disputes.* Disputes often arise between primes and subs over slowness of payments by primes which results in refusal to perform by

subs. Sometimes these disputes must be settled in court. One person suggested that there should be a limit to the amount of time that can lapse between presentation and solution of such disputes. Another stated that there should be one authoritative source of immediate resolution of payment problems. Caltrans itself is a source of disputes because it is difficult to obtain approval of "extras" from this agency.

5. *Skills/experience.* Most W/MBEs do not have the "know how" to bid large jobs and to perform successfully. However, firms currently performing on the Century Freeway appear to have this "know how." W/MBEs often do not adhere to all requirements of the contracting system. Lack of financial management ability causes 65% of all new contractors to fail annually in California. This is only a part of the problem. A variety of other business knowledge and skill areas are lacking in W/MBEs: knowledge of job cost tracking so that future projects may be estimated correctly; ability to manage cash flow; knowledge and ability to prepare paper work necessary for obtaining loans; understanding of their contractual arrangement with primes; training in management, accounting, expectations of prime contractors; understanding of the competitive bid procedure, including all costs of performance. These and other factors lead to under bidding by W/MBEs, primes taking advantage of this in order to secure contracts from Caltrans, and eventual substitution of W/MBE subs.

6. *Over extension of W/MBEs.* W/MBEs frequently contract for more work than they can successfully complete. They often cannot afford the payrolls and equipment rental costs if they are spread over several jobs. One suggestion was that they should not bid more than they can bond.

7. *Sources of assistance.* W/MBEs need a direct source of funding that will accept the contract as collateral, inasmuch as terms usually lock out funding for W/MBEs. One suggestion was that primes should assist with start up money. Also, primes should cover subs under their bond. Others state that general contractors have to spend too much time in assisting subs. There appears to be general agreement, however, that bonding and loan programs need to be expanded to allow more participation.

This ends the narrative illustration. The remaining outline follows, without the narrative for the Freeway Group:

B. The Role of CFTAP in Technical, Management, and Financial Assistance Provided to W/MBEs.

    1. *What CFTAP does.*

    2. *Evaluation of CFTAP.*

    3. *CFAAC/CFTAP relations.*

    4. *Change suggestions.*

    5. *Financing and financial management.*

     6. *Legal assistance.*

     7. *Funding.*

     8. *Use of services by W/MBEs.*

     9. *Prime/sub relationships.*

     10.   *The process of providing CFTAP services.*

C. The Main Causes of Substitution of W/MBE Subcontractors By Primes on the Freeway Projects, Including Appropriate Examples of Subcontractor Substitution.

     1. *Consent decree.*

     2. *Government agencies.*

     3. *Bidding.*

     4. *Business failure.*

     5. *Cash flow/financing.*

     6. *Delays.*

     7. *Disputes.*

     8. *Insurance/bonds.*

     9. *Performance.*

     10. *Prime/sub relations.*

     11. *Selection of W/MBEs.*

     12. *Subterfuge.*

D. Existing Mechanisms or Approaches For Resolution of Disputes Other Than Subcontractor Substitution Between Prime and Subcontractors on Freeway Projects

     1. *Causes of disputes.*

     2. *Contractual requirements.*

     3. *Relationships between primes and subs.*

     4. *Caltrans.*

     5. *Objectivity.*

     6. *Appeals and third party processes.*

     7. *Prime contractor assistance to W/MBEs.*

     8. *Technical assistance.*

E. Recommendations to Judge Pregerson and the Court

     1. *Consent decree.*

     2. *Disputes.*

     3. *Substitutions.*

     4. *Caltrans.*

     5. *CFTAP.*

     6. *CFAAC.*

     7. *Qualified W/MBEs.*

     8. *Technical assistance to W/MBEs.*

     9. *Training.*

     10. *Financing/bonding.*

Chapter 6

Case Two:
A County Personnel Department: Classification and Pay Division

Importance of the Study

While the study upon which this chapter is based was a routine consulting assignment which is described below, its importance for the CSM is that a comparison was made between data gathered using the method and interviews of key personnel. Thus, a qualitative comparison was provided by using two methods to ask two different groups of people from the same organization essentially the same questions. The important issue is: To what extent does the CSM produce approximately the same findings as are revealed using one-on-one interviews? If the findings correspond, this suggests a validation of the CSM, at least by using one alternative methodology. It also leads to the conclusion that the CSM not only produces equivalent results, but because of fewer resource requirements, it is more cost-effective.

Background

RJA Management Consultants was engaged by the Director of Personnel to conduct an administrative analysis of the Classification and Pay Division of the Personnel Department. Our concern in this case is with identification of problems and solutions. However, the broader assignment also involved identification of work standards, responsibilities, work flow and task analysis, past performance data, job analysis of staff, interpretation of data, and making recommendations.

Targets

Because this was a "fishing expedition" type of intervention, the initial target was phrased in general terms: "What are the operational problems of classification and compensation from both departmental as well as divisional perspectives?" The buzz group procedure was used with a follow-up target on recapitulating advice to management.

Aside from the above basic information gathering, we also used a target titled: "Questions about the Crawford Slip Method for Improving Productivity." This was done to peak interest in the method in hopes that the organization would seek to train their personnel to solve problems in the future. The target was accompanied by an answering of questions and some discussion.

We also introduced the Target "specific troublesome tasks and interactions for which step-by-step directions are needed on paper;" followed by "step-by-step directions for tasks or interactions," and "mutual aid in improving first drafts of procedures." Again, the idea was to interest the organization in developing its own self-improvement capability.

Working Groups, Constraints

Slip gathering was carried out in a two hour session involving twenty people of the Classification and Compensation Division and some operating departments. No limitations were placed on the intervention, except that more time was not available. More time would have been needed for real progress in performance improvement through procedures writing. The side-by-side comparison shown in the appendix resulted from a constraint. The president of the consulting firm wanted a check on the results of the CSM by comparing them with interview data.

Findings

As stated above, the focus of this chapter is the comparative analysis of findings using the CSM and interviews. This comparison is made in the side-by-side analysis in the Appendix which follows. While there is lack of correspondence on some issues, the results appear to show the same findings in general. Subtitles on the CSM side reveal the pattern of slip classification.

APPENDIX
COMPARATIVE ANALYSIS OF FINDINGS FROM THE CRAWFORD SLIP METHOD AND RJA PERSONAL INTERVIEWS WITH CLASSIFICATION AND PAY DIVISION AND SOME DEPARTMENTAL EMPLOYEES

CSM

Mission/Objectives

A mission statement for the Division needs to be identified in order for staff to have a broader perspective of what they can do for departments and what departments can expect of the Division. Objectives also need to be developed and communicated to operating departments.

RJA

Division Purpose/Mission

To maintain the integrity and equity of the Classification and Salary Plan for the County by conducting classification and salary studies, recommending actions consistent with the County's classification plan, resolving employee relations matters, and responding to classification and salary inquiries. It is the goal of the Division to provide quality centralized classification and salary services in a fair, timely, and economical manner.

Standards

Timelines need to be incorporated in goals and standards for the Division. Perhaps this will help the Division deal with studies submitted which do not warrant review, and having to deal with political decisions that are contrary to good personnel practice.

Guidelines and procedures are not available to ensure consistency and accuracy in the Division's work There is need for a continuous maintenance for both classification and pay plans. One person suggested that there

Standards

Most analysts reported that performance standards had never been provided to them. Three analysts provided performance evaluation guidelines describing results areas, job functions, and performance standards. These guidelines were provided to the analysts approximately five years ago and are used to guide the analyst in self-evaluation.

Standards that the Classification and Pay Analysts believed their work should be measured against included:

CSM	RJA
be two organizational units, one for maintenance of classification and pay plans, and the other for special projects and studies.	1. Quality

RJA (continued):

1. Quality
   a. thoroughness
   b. accuracy
   c. acceptability
      (1) number of revisions
      (2) clarifications
      (3) amplifications
      (4) fine tuning
2. Meeting deadlines
   a. processing Board referals within 30-45 days
   b. processing an average of one request per week for simple studies
   c. processing of complex, group studies, or re-definitions of series require more time
   d. responding within 60 days on status of a study
3. Working relationships
   a. intra-departmental (department staff)
   b. inter-departmental (liaison)
   c. consequences of advice
   d. positive or negative feedback
4. Other
   a. leadership skills
   b. number of studies
   c. mentoring
   d. diversity assignments
   e. grievance appeals
   f. grievance solutions

Management
Administrators in the Personnel Department in general could be

Management
Management is accepting studies that do not warrant review.

CSM	RJA
better communicators. Often, timely information is communicated late or not at all. The administration makes commitments for the unit without consulting those involved. Regular workload is often affected without informing the classification and pay analyst.	Management accepts studies before conferring with Classification and Pay Division staff.

Supervisor   *Supervisor*

The supervisor of classification and compensation was viewed as being generally unavailable and inaccessible. Some of the reasons suggested for this problem were: too broad a span of supervision, too many other responsibilities, too much time devoted to :putting out fires."

The Division chief is gone a lot assisting the Personnel Director.

The division chief is acting more as the Deputy Director.

The division chief's span of control has grown considerably, affecting her ability to respond quickly to staff questions.

Inability to talk to the division chief about studies.

Staffing

Personnel staffing ought to be brought to full complement. Especially needed is to fill the Assistant Director of Personnel position with someone skilled and knowledgeable in classification and pay issues. Otherwise,

CSM	RJA
there is need for a bridge class between supervisor and staff. This need is not being met by current use of senior class.	

Analysts
Several slips commented on need for additional analysts. Analysts feel themselves to be over worked and unable to give timely responses and to do high quality work because of the volume of workload.

Feedback	*Feedback*
Supervisor does not give feedback to subordinates on performance. The effect of this is to reduce motivation.	Analysts generally believed there was a great need to provide staff with feedback and recognition (good or bad). the lack of feedback and recognition has contributed to errors, caused analysts to spin their wheels, and perpetuated a number of problems.
It was suggested that set days and times to meet with the supervisor would be helpful. Bi-weekly staff meetings might be held. One person suggested the need for participatory management.	

Communication	*Communication*
There is need for better communication channels in the Department and the Division. Analysts feel that they are not being informed of what others are doing, and that this promotes duplication of effort. Lack of communication between Classification and Recruitment was mentioned.	There needs to be more sharing of information regarding the Department. Delays in feedback create and perpetuate problems. Lack of quick feedback causes analysts to waste time.

Workload	*Workload*
It was suggested that workload could be more evenly distributed	All analysts felt they had heavy workloads. One

CSM

among staff. Interruptions also result in uneven workload. An example given was special projects, such as salary surveys for outside agencies, which take away from time to complete classification studies. Senior staff members are required to perform analyst's duties not related to classification studies, such as cyclical employee relations work connected with negotiations. Personnel Depart needs work standards for various types of studies. A thorough review of workload and productivity should be undertaken. It should then be used to determine staffing requirements. One person observed that Classification and Pay staff members spend too much time in social interaction.

Calssification and Pay Technology
It was felt that changes in methods are needed. The Position Description Form is too long and complex, which delays departmental turn around time on the form. A shorter method of determining out-of-class work situations could be devised; salary could be adjusted before completion of the study. Alternative processes in general ought to be devised for routine classification studies. Perhaps the Position Description Form could be eliminated complet-ely in some cases inasmuch as the

RJA

analyst had a backlog of 15 studies, one requested as far back as 1984 (this study in 1986). Record keeping of studies in progress and completed, as well as required close-out procedures, tend to place added burden on the analysts. Routine surveys use up considerable analysts' time that could be spent on more important studies. Complex surveys and questions regarding comparability should be assigned to analysts, the remainder could be handled by clerical staff or a personnel technician.

Classification Methodology
One analyst described Position Description Forms as:
1. elaborate
2. time consuming
3. intimidating
4. an excellent tool for gaining greater insight into the job

Some departments have taken up to a year in completing and returning forms to the Personnel Department. Experienced analysts know when and when not to use the Position Description Form or, if

CSM

analysts conduct verbal interviews. Another suggestion was to involve analysts in departmental planning for new programs rather than developing the program and then calling Classification. Departmental representatives noted that it is very difficult for Personnel to understand specialized duties in the departments. Implications and issues of work at the operating level are often missed.

Staff does not have access to available reference information. For example, the ability to make comparisons with duties of similar job titles in other counties is limited.

Career Development and Training Needs

Many slips reported a need for staff training at all levels. Particularly needed is a program for new analysts and clerical personnel. Management support and encouragement of professional development activities for analyst staff is needed. At present there are limited career advancement opportunities for analysts.

Prioritization

Each analyst prioritizes his/ her own workload, but has

RJA

necessary, which parts to use. Problem is inexperience.

Several analysts expressed concern about the amount of time and effort expended in either gathering classification and salary information from or providing it to external county organizations. Comparison County information is outdated. It is time consuming to go through information that is poorly maintained.

Staff Experience and Training Needs

Inexperience and very little knowledge of personnel theory have created some problems in completing studies. Likewise, too long in one assignment and lack of promotional opportunities may be contributing to employee "burnout," thus affecting productivity and morale. Several analysts noted the need for more access to someone knowledgeable about classification and salary issues. While some inexperieneced analysts are assigned a mentor, others are not. Those not assigned a mentor have had to learn through trial and error.

Setting Priorities

All analysts expressed concern about the major delays caused

CSM

little control over the ultimate flow of work and time lines. There is frequent redirection and re-prioritization of work which results in delays to departments. Projects from the Board of Supervisors often cause changes in priorities. Some departments do not understand this. Departments themselves frequently re-prioritize their studies which causes delays in other work. It was suggested that the Division be authorized to set priorities for departments, taking departmental desires into consideration. Guidelines developed should help departments to understand prioritization. Studies with no deadlines often get lost. Delays in carrying out Division workload are also caused by the necessity to train new analysts and by interruptions from special Board of Supervisors requests.

Standard Formats
It was noted that the Division is a bit of a paper work "monster" which could be simplified. For example, standard formats for memoranda and letters could be devised.

RJA

by re-directions, unexpected interruptions, and the constant setting of new work priorities. Changes in priority often occur while the analyst is working on another study. Special projects, alone, may delay work several days.

Standard Formats
Each analyst is required to draft a two-page memorandum summarizing the facts and outcomes of the study. There is not a standardized format for this task, making it difficult to know what should go into the memo. Analysts generally agreed that the intent of the memorandum was good and would be useful to analysts in the future. However,

CSM   RJA

some analysts are not tracking as they
go, thus, lacking a standard format,
they have difficulty recalling what
they have done.
Other analysts believe that
this requirements uses
valuable time that could be
better spent on other
studies.

Clerical Assistance

Clerical Problems

The clerical support unit is
thought to be poorly organized.
Work performed by clerical
personnel is inadequate—
much proof reading and correct-
ing of errors is required. Some
clerks are weak typists.
Clerical processes hold up work
output. Several comments were
made on the need for a new technician class to perform lower
level technical duties.

Clerical problems identified
by several staff included:
1. difficulty in getting
documents back from
clerical staff in a
timely fashion
2. inaccuracy of typing
3. inordinate amount of
required re-typing
4. inadequate proof read-
ing of documents
5.Inexperience with word processing
system

Equipment/Automation

Equipment

There is a definite need to incorporate automated systems in
work processing. Classification
and compensation ought to be
computer assisted. The need
also extends to word processing
and reprographic equipment.
Reproducing copies consumes
considerable time.

The word processing equipment and photocopying mach-
ine are considered essen-
tial to increased efficiency
and productivity.

There is need for servicing
or replacing of typewriters.

Facilities and Working Area

Workspace

Physical office arrangements
make work difficult. Both
space and equipment are inadequate. Office space is crowded.

Inadequate space for clerical
staff.

CSM

Operating Department Abuses
The departments attempt to utilize the classification system to resolve personnel performance problems; for example, seeking to reward long-term employees through reclassification.

Departments use Personnel Department as the scapegoat for reclassifications they have already decided were invalid. Departments allow incumbents of positions to formulate requests for reclassification study of own positions. Form 11s are frequently submitted by departments without necessary background information. Departments do not consult with Personnel Department staff sufficiently in advance of major submittals. Constant change in organization structure in various departments increases workload by causing division staff to conduct organizational analyses and to formulate recommendations. Frequent requirements for re-study when departments do not agree with findings; most often the outcome is the same.

Communication With Operating Departments
A frequent reason for delays in meeting deadlines is lack of information. This is often caused by departmental slowness in responding to requests for

RJA

Operating Department Abuses
Lack of specificity in what is wanted or needed.

Changes in perceived needs.

Re-submission of previously denied requests for classification or reclassification. Normally, reclassifications incorporate job redesign.

Narrow interest in titles and salaries.

Inability to distinguish between a classification and organization study.

Communication With Operating Departments
Analysts repeatedly faulted operating departments for delays in completing studies. Slowness in providing Classification and Pay Division

| CSM | RJA |

CSM

information, often extending from nine months to two years.

Division personnel perceive that response time from operating departments for classification and salary data is extraordinarily long.

Specific delays in waiting for departmental data are experienced for position description forms.

Recruitment and Selection
Delays are also experienced in waiting for information from other divisions of the Personnel Department. For example, waiting for draft specifications to be returned with comments from Recruitment and Selection Division.

RJA

analysts with information required to commence, conduct, and/or complete a study have resulted in analysts setting aside or assigning lower priorities to indexed studies. Although most departments are remiss in providing information, generally, several analysts cited completion of the Position Description Forms as a serious problem.

Recruitment and Selection
Classification and Pay Division Analysts are required to submit classification specifications and proposed salaries directly to the Recruitment and Selection Division chief for review and approval. The review centers on appropriateness of minimum qualifications required of potential applicants and adequacy of recommended salaries in attracting qualified candidates. A number of analysts reported that lengthy delays occur in obtaining action from the Recruitment and Selection Division chief.

Chapter 7

Case Three:
Survey of Training Needs and Training Program Development for a Community Redevelopment Agency

Importance of the Study

This case is about development of a project manager training program for a community redevelopment agency of a major U. S. city. The CSM was used as the basic methodology for surveying training needs.

Background

The chief of operations and the deputy administrator for management services perceived that an important avenue to performance improvement in the agency was training. One of the authors was engaged to make the survey, design, and conduct the program with the assistance of subject specialists.

Initial meetings were held with the chief of operations and deputy administrator and, based on ideas discussed concerning staff deficiencies, a first draft of a program was developed. This is shown in the Appendix under the title: Tentative Schedule and Outline. Managers at the next, or third level, were to be interviewed.

Targets and Workshop Groups

Project managers and assistant project managers (22), the proposed trainees, were interviewed as a group using the CSM. Following presentation of the method a warm-up target was asked: "What are the operational problems of project management at the agency?" This was followed by a read back to ensure compliance with instructions.

The main data gathering target was: "What are your needs for training and development, as well as the needs of your counterparts, in order to do better project management at the agency?" This was followed by a buzz group and the follow-up target of: "Imagine yourself as the sole advisor to management on Targets A and B concerning problems and solutions; give your best advise." Slips from the first and last targets were merged, classified, and fed back to higher management under the title: "Problems and Improvements for the Agency as Suggested By Project Management Personnel." This report is omitted from the case.

Constraints and Modifications

Difficulties with availability of third-level management necessitated substitution of a questionnaire for interviews. Further, higher management suggested that some project management staff might have educational deficiencies which would inhibit learning in the training program. Thus, it was decided to develop a questionnaire which queried higher management on two areas: 1) a rating of basic educational development needs of each project manager and assistant project manager—reasoning, mathematical, and language development of these individuals using scales originally adapted by Sidney Fine for the Department of Labor[1]; and 2) ratings of learning objectives which were derived from the CSM intervention and discussions with management using the alternatives — don't know, not needed, marginal value, needed. The record on previous training was consulted and indicated on the questionnaire, as well.

Findings and Outcomes

Questionnaire results were tabulated and the training program was modified from the results. The revised training outline is shown in the Appendix as "Project Management Training Program - Schedule and Outline." Need for remedial basic education proved not to be a significant requirement.

APPENDIX
SURVEY OF TRAINING NEEDS
AND TRAINING PROGRAM DEVELOPMENT
FOR A COMMUNITY REDEVELOPMENT AGENCY

Project Management Training Program
Tentative Schedule and Outline

Meetings 1 - 4

1. The Environment of Public Management

The public; interest groups; political officials; bureaucracies; federalism and constitutionalism; intergovernmental relations; the policy formulation process; ethical conduct and the public interest.

The political economy of public organizations; production of public goods; monopolies and markets; efficiency and productivity.

Meetings 5, 6

2. Management in General

Organizing and matrix organization; accountability and control; organization culture; coordination; resources; management and the media.

Meetings 7 - 10

3. Human Resource Management in Matrix Organizations

Motivation, leadership, and human behavior in formal organizations; supervision, performance appraisal, discipline; administration of the MOU, grievance handling.

Meetings 11 - 15

4. Project Planning and Control

Statistical analysis fundamentals; sampling; network models; simulation; forecasting for planning and control; relationships to budgeting.

Meetings 16 - 20

5. Decision Making

Decision criteria; expected value; trees and tables; benefit-cost analysis; marginal analysis.

Meetings 21, 22

6. Software

Planning, control and decision making; project management information and decision support systems.

Meetings 23, 24

7. Program/Project Evaluation

Objectives and criteria; research design; monitoring and other data gathering systems.

Training Subjects
Rated as Needed/Not Needed
By Higher Management
The following subjects were identified in initial discussions and through the CSM as training needs. These subjects were then rated by higher management as needed (by at least 3 out of 4) or not needed. Number of personnel having received previous training was obtained from agency records.

Subject	*Training Needed*		Previous
	Yes	*No*	*Training*
1. *Environment of Public Management*			
Public/community interest groups & politics		x	
Political officials and bureaucracies		x	
Federalism and constitutionalism		x	
Policy formulation process	x		
Ethical conduct and the public interest		x	
Political economy of public organizations; production of public goods, monopolies and markets; efficiency and productivity		x	
Functions and requirements of other city departments and the city council	x		
Identify neighborhood problems and develop solutions	x		
Working with community leaders & groups; citizen participation groups	x		
Avoiding political pressure in making operations decisions	x		
2. *Matrix Management in General*			
Organizing and matrix organization	x		
Accountability and control	x		
Organization culture	x		
Coordination	x		
Resource management	x		
Management and the media	x		
How to analyze and improve administrative systems	x		
How to manage personal stress	x		6

Subject	Training Needed		Previous Training
	Yes	*No*	
How to manage one's time	x		4
How to delegate		x	1
How to develop a calendar of monthly events, reports, due dates, etc.	x		
3. *Human Resource Management in* Matrix Organizations			
Motivation and human behavior in formal organizations	x		4
Supervision and influence	x		4
Supervision: performance appraisal and discipline*	x		
Administration of the MOU and grievance handling*	x		*12
How to build team work	x		15
Dealing with multiple roles and role conflict	x		
Improving communications between operations and technical departments	x		
Position analysis for position design, selection, training, performance appraisal	x		
4. *Project Planning and Control*			3
Statistical analysis fundamentals		x	
Network models	x		
Simulation		x	
Forecasting for planning and control	x		
Budgeting and project management	x		
How to plan a project	x		
How to set goals and objectives	x		
Understanding pro forma cash flow analysis	x		8
Understanding accounting in a project driven organization	x		1
Determining and meeting staffing requirements in a matrix organization	x		
Establishing and managing priorities	x		
Understanding personnel system problems which relate to project managers	x		

Subject	Training Needed Yes	No	Previous Training
5. *Decision Making*			
Decision Criteria	x		
Expected value		x	
Trees and tables		x	
Benefit-cost analysis		x	
Marginal analysis		x	
6. *Software*			12
Planning, control, and decision making	x		
Project management information &			
decision support systems	x		
7. *Program/Project Evaluation*			
Objectives and criteria	x		
Research design		x	
Monitoring and data gathering systems	x		
8. *Other Personal Skills*			
Making speeches and other public			
presentations	x		3
Speed reading		x	
Running meetings efficiently	x		2
How to negotiate	x		2
9. *Other Technical Skills*			
Understanding the redevelopment			
process*			6
(other cities, redevelopment plan			
amendment process, technical tasks			
such as relocation, redevelopment			
law**)	x		**9
Current issues of redevelopment finance			
(federal and state low income tax			
credits, bankruptcy proceedings,			
minority-women's business enterprise			
procedures)	x		
Understanding urban planning	x		
Understanding California Environmental			
Quality Act (CEQA)	x		
Understanding environmental assessment	x		
Understanding real estate development			
principles	x		

| | Training Needed | | Previous |
Subject	Yes	No	Training
Understanding financing and creative financing of real estate agreements	x		
How to put together a real estate deal	x		

Project Management Training Program
Schedule and Outline

Meeting 1 - 4
1. *The Environment of Public Management*
    The policy formulation process; identifying and solving local/neighborhood problems; working with local interest groups.
Meeting 5
2. *Management in General*
    Organizing and matrix organization; accountability and control; organizational culture; coordination; resources; management and the media; improving administrative systems.
Meeting 6 - 11
3. *Human Resource Management in Matrix Organizations*
    Supervision, motivation, leadership; human behavior in formal organizations; performance appraisal and accountability; administration of the MOU, grievance handling; staffing in project management; and from the perspective of the project manager—building team work, roles and role conflict, communication with technical departments, delegation, time management, reducing personal stress.
Meeting 12 - 19
4. *Project Planning and Control*
    Planning projects—goals, objectives, timing, sequence; managing priorities; network models; forecasting for planning and control; sampling; relationships to budgeting and accounting; pro forma cash flow analysis.
Meeting 20 - 23
5. *Software*
    Planning, control, and decision making; project management information and decision support systems.
Meeting 24
6. *Program/Project Evaluation*
    Objectives and criteria; monitoring and other data gathering systems.

Chapter 8

Case Four:
Use of CSM in a Major State Agency to Surface Problems and Possible Solutions

Importance of the Study

There is an ongoing concern by governmental managers that their organizations are well administered. Managers wish to ensure that their organizations employ sound administrative management practices as they strive for organizational effectiveness and administrative efficiencies. Currently, this concern is most visible in efforts to "Reinvent Governments."

In launching reinvention efforts and instituting continuous improvement programs it is essential to become aware of perceived administrative problems and of the range of possible solutions seen by employees of the organization. The CSM is a useful tool for expeditiously surfacing those problems and solutions as is illustrated in the following case example.

Background

A USC team composed of one of the authors and three graduate students met with the Secretary of a large state agency and members of his staff to administer the Crawford Slip Method in an effort to identify problems the group perceived and possible remedies for those problems[2]. This meeting was a part of a broader study of approaches that might be taken to reinvent this particular agency.

Targets

The following was the first target for this workshop:
"WHAT ARE THE ADMINISTRATIVE OBSTACLES TO ACHIEVING EFFECTIVE PERFORMANCE BY YOUR AGENCY?"

The group was asked to respond in "ing" language meaning that they were asked to start each slip with a word ending in "ing" as they stated their problems. Some amplifying probes were used to further stimulate the thinking of workshop participants:

a. What constraints need to be revised or eliminated?

b. What laws are causing problems?

c. What government wide policies or practices need to be changed?

The second target was as follows:

"WHAT ARE SOME POSSIBLE PATHS OR SOLUTIONS TO OVER-COME THE ADMINISTRATIVE OBSTACLES IDENTIFIED UNDER TARGET A?

The group was asked to start each slip with an active verb as they indicated possible solutions. Additional directions used to guide their thinking were:

a. Select one of the obstacles you identified for target A.

b. Pick it for urgency in its need for improvement.

c. Give it a short title in "ing" language like you did for target A.

d. *UNDERLINE* it so it differs from the slips you will write about it in active verb language.

e. Then write slips starting in active verbs.

Workshop Groups

This workshop included the Agency Secretary and eight of his key staff. We were interested primarily in demonstrating the method to the Secretary and explaining how it could be employed on a larger scale with a defined research population such as a randomly drawn sample of Agency employees, or a vertically drawn sample representative of employees at certain organizational levels.

In this particular instance, by employing the Crawford Slip Method nine participants produced 59 problem statements in about twenty minutes. Then, the participants wrote slips for twenty minutes on possible steps to remedy *some* of these problems. The USC team subsequently classified the slips and performed minor editing on them in terms of format and style but not content. The classifications that emerged from perusal of the slips are: Relationships with the Governor's Office; Relationships with other agencies; Relationships with the federal government; Priorities of internal management; Internal communications; and Paperwork, equipment and staff procedures.

Constraints

The biggest constraints involved in this case was the small number of individuals included in the workshop. One implication for participants in this case is that they could readily see that by expanding the number of slip writers and including a broader sample of agency personnel a very informative report could be written with minimal time invested by Agency personnel.

APPENDIX
SURFACING PROBLEMS AND SOLUTIONS
IN A MAJOR STATE AGENCY

This appendix contains the body of the report provided to the Agency Secretary as feedback from the slip writing session. In essence these are the findings from the application of the CSM. The report has two objectives: 1) to provide the Secretary and his staff with an organized, classified set of slips that conveys substantive information on Agency problems and possible solutions; and 2) to illustrate the potential of the CSM if applied on a larger scale in the Agency.

Noted below will first be a listing of the problem statements written in "ing" language followed by possible ways of resolving some of the problems written beginning with action verbs. Crawford used this format to minimize the amount of editing required on slips while providing a relatively uniform language for readers of the report.

Problems identified with respect to relationships with the Governor's Office:

> Communicating with the Governor's Office
> Getting the Governor's Office to trust the agency more
> Responding to unrealistic time demands of the Governor's Office
> Conveying the Governor's message despite bureaucratic reluctance to change
> Getting timely responses from departments to permit prioritization of "emergency" requests from the Governor's office
> Responding too slowly to needs of the Governor's Office and staff
> (Not) anticipating adequately these needs

Possible *solutions* to some of the above problems:

> Encourage prioritization of action requests from the Governor's Office
> Determine a single contact point for "trafficking" action requests
> Get the Governor's Office to trust the agency more

Problems in relationships with other agencies:

> Eliminating the civil service system to improve motivation of department staff
> Reducing Agency size looks necessary given scope of Agency departments

Having Finance ask this Agency for a lion's share of general
fund cutting
Coordinating with several other governmental entities before
final policy decisions can be made
Developing better and more press opportunities
Dealing with duplicative government review/comment
procedures

Possible *solutions* to *some* of the above problems:
Consolidate government-wide review process so as to eliminate
as many steps as possible in current administrative/bureaucratic
procedures
Identify strategy for eliminating externally imposed obstacles
Obtain greater legislative and financial discretion over our
administrative spending
Identify a point person to meet with the department of Finance
frequently to better understand other side of issues;
same for the Governor's Office
Meet with cabinet office to design a plan for submitting
action requests to agency

Problems in relationships with the federal government:
Dealing with federal statutory mandates that limit the ability
of a state program to design or change social programs
Eliminating many federal laws affecting the states
Reimbursing the state for federal level policies on
immigration
Mandating practices of the federal government
Implementing federal mandates without funding
Dealing with federal statutes that inhibit state flexibility
to manage social programs
Improving immigration policies of the federal government

Possible *solutions* for *some* of the above problems:
Obtain administration-wide consensus that there is willingness
to propose a radical departure from the current joint
federal-state administration of agency programs
Equalize immigration problems among all states so the burden
is spread
Obtain reimbursement from the federal government for illegal
immigrants
Obtain waiver so we don't have to provide our services to
illegal immigrants

Change the 14th Amendment of the Constitution
Devise a list of options of how federal law could be changed
to better permit state discretion in the administration
of programs
Tighten up the borders of the United States
Choose one program in which federal statutory provisions are
excessively onerous in terms of state administration of
program
Offer up as an alternative the complete state withdrawal from
one of the major federal-state social programs
Assist counties in receiving federal reimbursement for illegal
immigrants

Problems with priorities of senior management:
Responding in a helpful way to our departments without being
a control agency
Getting top Agency staff focused on major policy initiatives
which is not always the "fun" stuff
Failing to observe the larger context of a specific problem
Duplicating review and comment activities associated with
policy proposals

Possible *solution* steps for *some* of the above problems:
Imagine the worst possible program outcome and how it would
be quantified
Try to imagine practical measures/scales which permit
quantification
Imagine the best possible outcome and direct or proxy measures
of that outcome
Break it down to several related measures if possible and
focus on the timing of useful measures

Problems with internal communications:
Not knowing the Secretary's priorities well
Keeping everyone up to speed on larger decisions/events within
the Agency
Spending an inordinate amount of time in meetings
Eliminating the endless meetings
Reducing meetings to increase time for development of
products
Communicating better among management staff
Better communications with the Department of Finance
Improving communications among Agency staff so that all of us
are on the same "page"

Assuring organizational stability—processes change quickly;
changes often are not communicated clearly; not
documented for later use

Communicating within various "units" of the Agency; i.e.,
press, legislative, policy/fiscal, Secretary's office

Getting communications to flow from department directors to
appropriate staff

Getting accurate information from departments

Possible *solutions* to some of the above problems:

Increase contact with the Secretary so that his goals and
priorities are known and can be responded to

Meet with the Chief Deputy Directors on a regular basis and
provide them key information

Hold regular Director's meetings at least every two weeks

Stress to the Directors the importance of communicating *all*
the way through departmental staff

Get communications to flow from Agency to the department
staff through the Directors

Use memos from the Secretary or Undersecretary on really
important issues

Provide Departments with more information as the reasons for
rush requests

Problems with trust within the Agency:

Getting top level Agency staff to trust and utilize expertise
of Assistant Secretaries more

Encouraging more team participation among Directors

Getting better participation from Departments

Allowing Departments greater latitude in allocating
administrative expenses

Possible *solutions* to *some* of the above problems:

Have the Secretary tell the Directors on a one-on-one basis in
meetings about problems which have risen and hold the
Directors accountable for them

Improve trust and communication with more one-on-one
contact

Establish a policy to involve Assistants on issues when those
issues first come up

Delegate more

Delegate non-sensitive items to Departments; i.e., conferences
held internally for purposes of training staff

Determine ways to involve the whole office (support staff too) in feeling like a team

Build an organization for the long-term. . .beyond when individual staff members depart

Clarify unclear areas and empower appropriate levels to make decisions

Reward/recognize good performance

Allow for the participation of multiple departments on specific issues

Communicate expectations clearly

Provide feedback to staff on an ongoing basis

Problems with paperwork, processes, equipment and staff:

Reducing paperwork possibly through automation

Working with the massive paper load

Reading massive amounts of reports/plans

Understanding how to move paper around the office in the most timely manner

Improving paper tracking and filing system so staff can easily locate documents

Making the workload manageable

Getting reports and assignments processed in a timely manner

Getting information and documents processed correctly from the departments

Clarifying unclear decision making authority within the Agency; e.g., Who signs? Who decides?

Overcoming obscure, unclear reporting relationships within the Agency. Who is reporting to whom on what issues?

Eliminating duplicate or triplicate approvals of documents within the agency

Discriminating between practical obstacles to implementation of the administration's policies and bureaucratic stonewalling

Developing interim measures of long-term program performance; for example, monitoring of achievements of preventive programs

Identifying appropriate performance measures

Getting the departments to complete routine tasks correctly and on time—like the week ahead report

Eliminating categorical reporting requirements for programs so that reporting can be integrated

Ceasing to use outdated, inefficient office equipment

Automating functions within the Agency

Working with old and inefficient office equipment-computers
Having enough support staff to complete work effectively
Dealing with overload—too much paper, too many demands,
same people working on the issues
Improving quality of staff in our departments—particularly
management so that Agency staff do not have to re-write
documents, etc.
Organizing clerical duties
Getting some support staff to happily do work

Possible *solutions* to *some* of the above problems:
Make better use of electronic mail
Produce ability to receive memos/information on-line in
document format—not just through the mail system
Provide modern capabilities on a few computers so we can
easily access outside information sources
Acquire the same computers for all staff and have linkage
capabilities
Hook everyone up to electronic servers so that information can
easily and readily be accessed—especially by support
staff
Increase tools and use of automation
Provide course for people who want to learn how to use their
system so they don't need to constantly ask questions and
get technical assistance, and have support staff do
"difficult" work
Reduce need for information and report review
Eliminate paperwork
Form a system that would include a one page summary or page
of bullets for each report or study distributed in the
office/agency
Form a working relationship that shares the burden of paper
pushing between the support staff and the executive staff
Form a system that includes route slips
Clarify decision making authority
Discriminate between real obstacles and bureaucratic
stonewalling
Require clear explanation of obstacles
Eliminate those obstacles
Determine which obstacles are controlled internally
(prioritization, workload distribution) and which are
imposed externally (court decisions, federal laws)
Remove the internally imposed obstacles

Establish ways/times to evaluate organizational processes
regularly and modify them as needed to assure performance
Document "existing" processes and authority; identify areas
of weakness and strength in Agency performance
Recognize Departments for achievements; hopefully cause them
to take more pride in successful outcomes
Improve obscure/unclear reporting within agency
Route *all* issues/*all* paper through deputy secretary who then
determines whether to forward to undersecretary
Make assistant secretaries responsible for policy issues; not
press or other staff
Identify staff roles more clearly. What do all these folks
do?
Obtain specific guidelines as to what documents and reports
are essential for further review and which ones are not

Chapter 9

Case Five:
Use of CSM in Intervening in a Training Program for a Federal Agency

Importance of the Study

In conducting training on management related topics such as changing organizations, continuous improvement, etc. It is not unusual to find some inattention or even resistance to the training objectives. When trainers sense that they are dealing with a hostile or angry group that needs to let off some steam, one effective way to do that without an unduly disruptive digression is to employ the Crawford Slip Method to facilitate the needed catharsis and at the same time produce some valuable data and insights into the sources of the anger. The CSM is a useful tool for surfacing problems and concerns; individuals who write slips do so anonymously and are usually candid in expressing themselves.

Background

During a one week training session on Leadership and Ethics for the 1990's, the Crawford Slip Technique was introduced to the group as a tool for mobilizing brainpower quickly in group settings. It was also introduced as a safe and efficient way to voice deeply felt problems and concerns.

One of the authors and another USC Professor were conducting a training program for 25 senior civilian and military leaders when they sensed the group was distracted and "up tight" about the current situation in their organization. The professors decided to employ the CSM to release the group's pent up feelings.

Targets

In less than one half hour the group wrote slips on two targets in what amounted to an impromptu workshop. The first target was to identify problems or concerns of group members vis a vis their organization in "How to" language. The second target was to recommend actions to address those problems or concerns by writing short statements beginning with an action verb.

The above mentioned slips were classified and are presented below. The classification was performed by the author. He reproduced the slips as written within his classification categories which were derived from a model of organizations as social systems composed of a set of interdependent variables; namely, structure, technology, resources, ideologies, strategies, relevant factors in the external environment, and the internal organizational climate. These categories best reflected his assessment of the major clusters of concerns derived from an analysis of the slips. As such, the categories provided a theory based "lens" for classifying and analyzing the slips.

Workshop Group

The 25 individuals in this training program were high level civilian and military leaders/managers who were caught up in the vortex of post cold war downsizing. The leadership training program had among its objectives the building of trust and teamwork among these higher echelon employees. While it had not set out to be a problem surfacing and solution raising effort, use of the CSM moved it in that direction and subsequent to the seminar the classified slips became the bases for follow up management problem solving sessions.

Constraints

The biggest constraint in this case was the impromptu use of the CSM. There was little time for setting targets and developing motivational orientation materials. This was very much a spontaneous application of CSM; it did not involve as much attention to "preventive editing" and required somewhat more effort to produce useful results.

APPENDIX
INTERVENING IN A TRAINING PROGRAM

Leadership Problems and Concerns:

How to improve shared leadership between military and civilians

How to improve the civilian/military working relationship

How to enhance the potential for shared leadership

How to reduce antagonism between civilian and military

How to cope with the fact that the military infrastructure has vested interests and actively, but quietly works to prevent civilians from assuming leadership positions

How to reconcile the desire to enhance military careers vice civilian expertise

How to ensure that civilian managers that have reached an important level of responsibility are not replaced by a military officer when the next military boss comes along

How to convince the civilian force that more civilian leaders are really desired

How to increase the role of civilians in the decision making process

How to make civilians valuable team members, or as valued as the military

How to have better working relations between the military and civilians

How to improve working relationships between military and civilian workforce (perceived second class citizenship of civilians)

How can the military leadership demonstrate that they are serious when saying they want civilians in key leadership roles

How can better feelings be created between military and civilians

How to enhance credibility of professional civilians in the "blue suit" environment

How to increase the role of civilian management in an essentially military environment

How to improve equality of status/treatment/job availability for military and civilians

How to promote equalitarianism between military and civilians

How to show civilians that they can contribute at a leadership level

How to obtain additional leadership (program manager) positions for civilians

How to achieve a stronger role for civilians
How to have more civilian leadership positions
How to remove constraints from civilian managers to enable
their making effective decisions
How to ensure a strong civilian base
How to eliminate the glass ceiling on the positions that can
be held by civilians (military still sit on all key
positions and executive level positions are virtually
nonexistent)
How to break the glass ceiling for women
How to break down military/civilian barrier system

Leadership Recommendations:

Lead by example, emphasize goals/mission then support
accomplishments
Encourage new ideas; support discussions and be open to
recommendations
Recommend streamlined management approaches and philoso-
phy; encourage and support by actions
Demonstrate seriousness to include civilians in leadership
roles by converting positions from military to civilian
Establish key leadership positions for civilians (in the
program and staff offices and at the corporate level)
Establish senior civilian leadership positions—NOW
Train and develop top civilians. Create civilian leadership
positions
Provide training to the civilian sector on teamwork
Allow the TQ teams to function as they determine vice
dictating such things a metric a month. Cut down the
associated bureaucracy
Be flexible
Get ideas from other sources (other than traditional)
Avoid quick judgements
Don't lean on previous experience
Reduce intervention - quit saying how things should be done;
be less judgmental
Reduce demands on organization
Accept I don't know as a good or even best answer
Focus on product, not format, polish, etc.

Communication Problems and Concerns:

How to improve communications and coordination between the
military and civilian leadership

How to get broader civilian representation on the Senior Leadership Council

How to establish a communication conduit from the civilian leaders and managers to the Commander

How to enable civilian managers to communicate and share concerns

How to create an atmosphere where civilians and military feel encouraged to raise issues up the chain for resolution

How to provide a more accurate portrayal of reality to senior management

How to ensure the voices of civilian managers are heard

How to develop a method of General Manager (GM) interchange horizontally

How to improve communications within the GM's

How to improve communications between military and civilians

How to create forums for interaction among middle managers (a number of forums exist for communication among top management)

How do we provide feedback on new/changing policies/ directions to assist senior level in evaluating success/programs of changes

How to let personnel know why changes are being made

How to assist the leadership in turning speeches into action

How to give proper voice to civilian middle management concerns

How to end prejudice in military - collective management roles

Communication Recommendations:

Provide for input to the top level executive board from the civilian management community which presently is voicing only one senior civilian view

Provide a forum for civilian/military managers for exchanging views and suggestions

Develop improved dialogue between military and civilian managers on civilian management concerns

Develop an effective forum for dialogue

Change the way programmatic information is provided senior management(Commander and Vice Commander); make less formal and more candid

Show some trust; limit justification needed to support recommendations

Avoid allowing staffs to overly filter or review input

Address both civilian and military concerns in base
publications, Commander Calls, etc.
Establish a method for GM's to communicate with commander
Create a civilian vehicle for all GM's to exchange
information, communications, ideas, etc.
Establish a GM organization at SSD to improve
communications
Establish a mid-level "off site" for GM/14/15 and LtC/Col
level to review cross organizational issues. Exclude the
two letters/ O-6 level; allow this group to collectively
provide feedback to the Commander
Increase communication among the various program offices and
civilian managers
Develop an organization for sharing information among mid-
level managers; empower this group to make recommendations.
Elevate issues to senior management. This group could be
civilian issues focused and be comprised of both civilian
and military mid-level managers
Provide required, frequent feedback sessions for all personnel
so that they may gain insight and a better understanding
of the magnitude and quality of their work
Assign a senior civilian ombudsman

Human Resources (Careers and Pay) Problems and Concerns:
How to improve career paths for civilian managers
How to improve career progression for civilian GM's
How to improve the satisfaction of being a manager (GM series)
given the unrealistic and restrictive appraisal system
which the Department uses
How to improve the rating and merit pay bonuses for civilian
GM's
How to return the civilian GM rating and reward system to an
equitable basis
How to improve the GM rating system
How to ensure civilian managers are recognized

Human Resources Recommendations (Careers and Pay):
Look after and promote the careers of civilians the way we do
military
Nurture and provide opportunities for civilian managers to
move ahead
Provide job enlargement and job enhancement opportunities so
that both civilian and military personnel can gain
experience and fill key positions (for example, cross

training in other functions, offices, etc.)

Provide better awards and recognition to GM"s

Once a GM is in a position, that GM should not be removed simply because of a new program director has a military person he has worked with/knows

Change GM appraisal system to accomplish the following: 1) revoke linkage of ratings with specified "bonus" amounts; 2) increase the bonus pool to provide a real incentive to GM's, etc., etc.

Overhaul GM rating system so that ratings are not tied to availability of funds

Eliminate artificial curve on GM/GS performance appraisals and acquire reasonable pay pool (5% - 10% of salaries)

Create an adequate civilian performance award pool so that the amount does not restrict the number of outstanding awards that can be given

Triple or quadruple the GS "bonus" pool to allow managers to truly reward employees who make significant contributions (individual or part of the team) so that people will see some tangible reflection of their efforts

Promote more women to upper management positions, recognizing existing untapped capabilities

Recognize that women are not being recognized for what they can do, their potential, and promote accordingly

Only topics and recommendations are listed to summarize the remainder of the report.

Human Resources (TQM, Training and Development) Problems and Concerns

Human Resources - Recommendations (Training and TQM)

Structural Problems

Recommendations on Structure

Organizational Climate/Environment, Problems

Organizational Climate and Environment, Recommendations

Goals, concerns

Goals - Recommendations

Resources - Problems and Concerns

Resources - Recommendations

Systems and Technologies - Problems and Concerns

Systems and Technology - Recommendations

Chapter 10

Case Six:
Survey of Experts on Earthquake Mitigation Management for Harbors and Seaports

Importance of This Study

This is an example of use of the Crawford Slip Method as one among three methods in an applied research project. The CSM was used as a data gathering approach at a conference of experts on the subject of effective earthquake mitigations in U. S. Pacific Basin harbors and seaports[3]. Other methods in the study included: case studies of Alaska, 1964, and Chile, 1960, earthquakes and subsequent developments; and a questionnaire survey of seaport mitigation management practices in Pacific Basin seaports and harbors.

Background

The broad objectives of this research were to provide information to seaport/harbor managers on what is and is not known about preoccurrence earthquake mitigations, the extent to which they have been applied and their general efficacy. More specifically, the research sought answers to the following questions:

1. What are problems and mitigations arising from seaport destruction and damage caused by earthquake-related phenomena?

2. What have been the nature and extent of damage, types of problems faced, the wider economic and social effects, and the planning, recovery and repair mitigations taken after the disasters?

3. What was the efficacy of mitigations? What actions were omitted; what alternatives were neglected; and what consequences were ignored?

4. What guidelines may be supplied to seaport/harbor management?

5. How practical do experts view this guidance to be? What important problems, effects, etc., have been omitted, and, therefore, what is expert opinion on action that might have been taken?

This case focuses on the last question but was influenced by the other queries, findings on which were reported at the conference. A literature search, was also a major part of the study. The literature survey resulted in development of a conceptual framework, as well as substantive information on earthquakes. The framework was used for developing the research questions as well as understanding and interpreting findings.

Targets and Workshop Group

Findings were derived from a one day conference on the subject of "Seismic Mitigation Management for Ports and Harbors" held at the Board Room of the Port of Los Angeles, on May 23, 1985. Forty seven persons were in attendance. Attenders represented: seaport engineering, planning and environmental staffs, port lessees; other local government officials; persons from universities and the construction industry.

Conferees were asked to write slips on their ideas about the seismic preparedness of U. S. Pacific Rim seaports. Next, following a buzz session, they were asked to describe their thinking on appropriate public policy initiatives, at all levels of government, to facilitate seaport seismic mitigation management. Data from these targets were combined and classified by the author.

Constraints

The main constraint on the CSM was that the conference was not solely built upon use of this methodology. Several experts presented papers on technical issues relevant to the subject. Attenders were probably most interested in these presentations. Thus, CSM data gathering was an intervention which ended the day.

Findings and Outcomes

The research report is too complex to summarize, but analysis of the slips gathered at the conference is recapitulated in the Appendix as major titles under which the narrative report was written. In addition to extensive distribution of the final report to seaport/harbor and seismic issue interested persons, as required by the National Science Foundation, a professional journal and a newspaper article resulted from the research[4].

APPENDIX
SEISMIC MITIGATION MANAGEMENT FOR PORTS
AND HARBORS
A MASS INTERVIEW OF CONFERENCE PARTICIPANTS

The following are major titles under which: 1) data were classified from participants writing slips on the target of seismic preparedness of U. S. Pacific Rim seaports; and 2) following a buzz session, participant thinking on appropriate public policy initiatives.

Vulnerability of Structures
Vulnernability of the Los Angeles/Long Beach Ports
Examples of Seaport Concern For Seismic Vulnerability
Government Problems
Economic Problems
Research Needs
Political Strategy and Constraints
Planning and Coordination
The Role of the Federal Government
Mitigations
Legislative Requirements

Chapter 11

Case Seven: Writing Contracting Procedures for the Tactical Air Command

Importance of this Study

In Chapter Three the technique of procedures writing using the Crawford Slip Method was discussed. Here problem solution is approached through procedures writing and consensus building. It should be remembered that procedures involve step by step descriptions (like cookbook recipes) of what needs to be done in order to achieve the objective or to solve the problem. Procedures writing may follow a "troubles and remedies" session in which tasks to be described, areas in need of improvement or consensus on what should be done emerge. Thus, the importance of this case is that it illustrates the CSM applied in a procedures writing mode.

Background

In 1979 a conference on contracting was called by the U. S. Air Force Tactical Air Command, Directorate of Contracting, headquartered at Langley Air Force Base in Virginia. Difficulties to be corrected resulted from the arcane nature of regulations governing contracting. These resulted in inconsistent actions by officials. John Demidovich, a Professor of Management at the Air Force Institute of Technology, was a conference facilitator. He concluded after a day or two that the experience would not produce useful results if something different wasn't done. He contacted C. C. Crawford with whom he had worked on many occasions. Demidovich frequently collected data using the CSM and usually asked Crawford to classify them. Dr. Crawford visualized a procedures writing approach. Within a day he was on site at Langley Air Force Base.

Targets and Workshop Group

Attenders at the conference included 90 persons of various Air Force ranks as well as civilian contracting employees from throughout the country and abroad. The 90 people had different kinds of special duties, therefore each individual was asked to select his or her own troublesome tasks on which to write procedures to guide his or her successor. The 90 persons had been pre-selected for this conference, to cover all the specialties and Air Force bases in representative ways.

By choosing tasks on which each one's successor would need help, there was a good prospect of covering the whole range of tasks fairly well. Each chose a task for the first procedure draft by two criteria: a) troublesome to a successor; b) Well known to the writer. It was expected that there would be more than one set of procedures for each of a few tasks by the end of the second morning. These duplications were clustered together and returned to slip writers the third morning, where the best were selected, or in some cases good features were merged. You remember from Chapter Three that part of the process includes a mutual aid editing function as different individuals review procedures, make comments and recommendations, and in some cases, negotiate appropriate statements.

Constraints

The greatest constraint on this project was that only three mornings were available to gather and agree upon procedure statements. This was mitigated to some extent through the work of a smaller group of eight persons who worked with Dr. Crawford during non-meeting times to become more sophisticated in the methods and to edit the work of the larger group. This is the group which identified duplicate versions of procedures.

Another constraint is really a problem of training people in the method. It is the difficulty in distinguishing tasks from problems. This is not unlike asking for problems and getting solutions instead; or, vice versa in asking for solutions. As stated in earlier chapters, one way to solve a problems is to write a procedure statement for its solution. However, in this case the tasks should have been known as given. The variables were: a) a clear understanding of steps to be taken; b) appropriate wording of procedure steps; and c) the proper sequencing of steps. Dr. Crawford's group of eight helpers culled problem statements and also clustered different versions of procedures for the same task.

Obviously, the anonymity factor was abandoned in this process. Names were signed for reasons of professional accountability and also as an aid to intercommunication as drafts were improved and refined while in the slip stage.

Findings and Outcomes

The group of 90 did finish its work in three mornings, supplemented by the editing of the subgroup of eight under Dr. Crawford's tutelage. One staff support person of the Directorate was instructed in Dr. Crawford's requirements for typing and formatting. Final details were worked out by mail.

Some samples of procedures from *TAC Contracting Procedures Guide*, the product of conference attenders, are shown in the Appendix. Indicative that this was well done is the fact that other commands adopted and reprinted the manual for use in their own contracting.

APPENDIX
SAMPLE CONTRACTING PROCEDURES

The following are samples of procedures from different parts and chapters of the *TAC Contracting Procedures Guide*, Tactical Air Command, Directorate of Contracting, Langley AIr Force Base, Virginia, 1979.

Three Sets of Procedures:

PART I. MANAGEMENT

CHAPTER I. ADMINISTRATION

1. Standardizing staff meetings
a. Establish regular schedule for staff meetings
b. Have meeting chaired by chief or deputy chief
c. Record minutes of meeting
d. Persons attending will be branch chiefs or others as authorized
e. Branch chiefs will give status on their branches
f. Branch chiefs will present status report to include command interest items, problem areas, response to information requests
g. Distribute minutes of meeting

2. Writing letters
a. Write down purpose of letter
b. Write down main points supporting purpose of letter
c. Place main points in logical sequence
d. Using main points write topic sentences for paragraphs in body of letter
e. Write examples supporting main points and group them under applicable main points
f. Write last sentence of each paragraph so it allows smooth, easy transition into next paragraph
g. Write closing paragraph which states what action you expect of reader or what action you will take
h. Keep letter brief; use plain English
i. Does letter answer questions: who, what, where, when, how, why?

3. Standardizing/improving documentation
a. Write date and location conversation or meeting was held
b. Reference document being discussed
c. Write down name of individual who initiated conversation or meeting
d. Write down names, organization, and telephone numbers of all participants
e. Write purpose of conversation or meeting
f. Write reasons you feel conversation or meeting is necessary
g. Write examples which support purpose for meeting
h. Write resolutions of conversations or meetings
i. Be sure appropriate signatures are obtained, when required

j. Make distribution of minutes, if required

k. Suspense action items of conversation or meeting, if required

Four Sets of Procedures:
PART II. SYSTEMS
CHAPTER 1. ADMINISTRATIVE
1. Processing incoming correspondence

a. Separate correspondence into stacks for registered mail and regular mail

b. Process registered mail first by date-stamping each envelope

c. Open each registered item not identified as invitation for bid response and date-stamp enclosed correspondence

d. Retain envelope when necessary; staple to contents

e. Distribute to appropriate office

f. Open envelopes of regular mail and date-stamp contents

g. Discard envelopes not other wise needed

h. Distribute to appropriate office

2. Establishing effective suspense systems

a. Establish 31 file folders - one for each day of the month

b. Obtain AF form 388 or similar form for any correspondence requiring suspense

c. Determine person(s) responsible for response or action

d. Complete AF form 388

e. Staple original copy of AF form 388 to document requiring action or response

f. Forward document to applicable person(s)

g. File copy of AF form 388 in appropriate folder

h. Initiate follow-up if response not received by suspense date

3. Accounting for procurement identification numbers (PIIN) - *purchase/delivery orders*

a. Review most recent purchase and delivery order register

b. List any PIINs not present in sequentially listed register

c. Compare list of missing PIINs to previous purchase and delivery registers

d. Refer to manual PIIN assignment logs to determine when PIIN was signed out or not used

e. Locate folders of PIINs that should have been reported

f. Verify keypunch (KP) date on routing sheet to be sure that order has not been processed in interim between last reporting cycle

g. Determine cause for failure to computer process award information

h. Make any necessary corrections to KP award document

i. Resubmit award input cards in next computer processing cycle

4. Monitoring priority abuse

a. Compare percentage of priority requisitions (priority 1-8) to routine

b. Review monthly reports to identify customers who exceed priority rate goal

c. Communicate priority ratio to customers who exceed priority rate goal

d. Obtain information on customers' circumstances that contribute to excessive percentages

e. Instruct buyers and supervisors to retain examples of suspected priority abuse

Chapter 12

Case Eight:
Development of a Transit Resource Center[5]

Importance of the Study

A bureaucrat challenged by the struggles of turning visions into realities, of involving stake holders, and gaining support for a new project decided that the Crawford Slip Method, a mass intervention process, would support the objectives. The expectation of the mass intervention was to gather pertinent information regarding: vision, mission, and goals for the Transit Resource Information Center. This study is an example of the versatility of the CSM, illustrating its usefulness not only to marshal the ideas of people but to develop a new program while involving stake holders and gaining support for the project.

Background

Because of California's blueprint, and the Intermodal Surface Transportation Efficiency Act of 1991 (ISTEA) whose principal aim is to "Develop a national Intermodal transportation system . . . and to increase mass transit programs," the requirements for Caltrans' involvement in rail and transit activities are increasing. Many within Caltrans want local governments and planning organizations to continue to maintain the lead in transit development. However, Caltrans through the Division of Mass

Transit perceives a need to provide information support and training in surface and rail transit related issues. For this reason, the Transit Resource Center (TRC) is being developed.

According to Rennie Adam, Chief of the Division of Mass Transportation, "The Transit Resource Center responds to Caltrans' policy to expand its partnership role by providing training and informational assistance in transit related issues to Caltrans' Districts and transit agencies." Transit agencies, in this context, are defined as: local transit authorities, regional transit authority, and regional transportation planning agencies.

Target and Working Groups

Turning visions into reality requires a plan and a process. For this purpose, this bureaucrat held a CSM workshop within Caltrans' Division of Mass Transit. The workshop was attended by 31 individuals at headquarters, Sacramento, California. There were two workshops, each 90 minutes long. The first workshop consisted of the Division Chief and Seniors. The purpose of the targets noted below was to identify and prioritize a strategic plan and process for the Center.

The second group consisted of Seniors and Transportation planners, who would be direct customers of the Center. The targets for this group, as noted below, sought to identify categories of transit information, quality standards, and ways to overcome cross functional and organizational barriers in order to exchange information. To enhance participant interest, during this session, the bureaucrat utilized buzz groups.

Each session began with an overview of the agenda to calm any anxiety participants may have had regarding the mass interview process. The agenda was divided into five steps. The first step defined the purpose or focus of the meeting. The second step was an overview of the Transit Resource Center concept and development. The third step explained the Crawford Slip Method. The fourth step, gave an explanation of buzz groups; and, finally, the last step assured everyone that there would be sufficient time for questions and answers at the end of the meeting regarding the CSM.

During the first step, the bureaucrat wrote a meeting mission statement for everyone to see. "Our mission today is to conceptualize what type of services the TRC should provide and identify the important topics and sub-categories that TRC information center should maintain." This pep talk, was encouraging and identified the importance of excellence. This step ended with a quotation from Aristotle, "We are what we repeatedly do. Excellence, then, is not an act, but a habit."

Next, the bureaucrat explained the importance of the participants' involvement and the need for their input to identify the vision and mission for the information center. During this time, the bureaucrat explained that CSM was part of a continuous improvement process (an open system) whereby their views and comments would be continually welcomed. Further, it was explained that this intervention was one of a series of CSM meetings to be held throughout the department and district offices. During this step, the bureaucrat provided an overview of the Transit Resource Center development phases and explained how this was phase one, the concept phase. Therefore, their assistance in designing the service was important because this phase requires their technical imagination and understanding of the transit industry.

In the next step the bureaucrat explained the workshop procedure and its safety, anonymity, and privacy. The participants were asked to be as clear and concise as possible. An emphasis was placed on the need for independent responses. At the conclusion of this step, the bureaucrat provided a short biography on C. C. Crawford.

During the last two steps the bureaucrat explained the use of buzz groups and assured everyone that there would be a question and answer session at the end.

Target Questions

The first group, which consisted of the Division Chief and Seniors, was asked the following questions:

1. What is your vision for the TRC Information Center?
   -What are the significant tasks TRC should be involved in?
   -What are the important things TRC should do well?
   -What higher standard than efficiency, should TRC incorporate in their decision making process?
2. What should TRC accomplish?
   -What type of services should be provided?
   -What has to be done to make TRC work?
   -Imagine an initial customer contact. What will make that customer tell his or her neighbors and associates that TRC is outstanding?
3. What transit related information should the center maintain in electronic and hard copy form for rapid accessibility?
   -What major topics should the information center contain both in electronic and hard copy?
   -What are the hot topics?
   -Please use technical terms and be specific.
4. Who do you believe can best be served by TRC?
   -Who should TRC partners and customers be?
   -Who would best benefit from transit information?

5.   How can TRC best serve you?
        -What types of services should TRC provide to assist you at
        your job?
        -Which services are most important to you?

The second group, which consisted of Seniors and transportation planners, was asked:

1.   What are the possible hindrances TRC will encounter when
        trying to gather and exchange information within DMT?
        -What are the 20% of barriers that cause 80% of the
        difficulties?
        -What have you observed or heard about?
        -What do different groups complain about (districts, planners,
        agencies)?

2.   How can these hindrances be prevented or remedied?
        -What should TRC do?
        -What should TRC not do?

3.   The next question is in two parts:
        FIRST: Identify what transit related information should the
        center maintain in its data base and reference center.
         -What major topics should the information center contain both
        in electronic and hard copy?
         -What are the hot topics?
         -Please use technical terms and be specific.

        SECOND: For each major category identified, what sub-
        categories, within your area of responsibility, should the
        information center maintain?
        -Identify those sub-categories that would be useful to you

BUZZ GROUP QUESTION

4.   How can TRC best serve you?
        -Separate into groups of three for 15 minutes.
        -No leader, no recorder, and no votes are to be taken.
        -Going clock-wise, each individual, one at a time, without
        interruption, briefly states his or her best thought on the
        subject.
        -After all have had an opportunity to state their ideas, the
        group will participate in a free-for-all discussion of the
        subject. This will continue for about 15 minutes. Then, we
        will return.
         -When we return, I will ask you to sum up your individual
        ideas.

When the buzz groups returned, the following statement was made: You are the sole consultant regarding TRC service. Write slips on the actions you recommended. I urge you to give your own views, not a summary of the thoughts of others. Please identify the best way TRC can serve you. I do not want the group's perspective; I want your individual point of view.

Findings and Outcomes

The workshop produced 426 slips that identified over 852 separate ideas or suggestions. The bureaucrat categorized these slips by topic. The following categories were not predetermined but emerged as a result of slip classification.
1. Vision
2. Service
3. Quality
4. Information

The slips grouped under the topic of *vision* identified the overall task and its large significance to the department and its customers.

The slips grouped under the topic of *service* provided specific examples of action steps that could be a part of the Center's strategic plan. The plan includes goals and criteria for roles and responsibilities in each phase. It reflects an emphasis on vision, service, and quality.

The slips grouped under the topic of *quality* set the quality level of services and determined what the quality features would be.

The slips grouped under the topic of *information* identified twelve major categories of information with over 51 sub-categories including 350 topics for the development of a data base and a lending library for transportation planners and transit operators throughout the State of California. The identification of pertinent information is critical because there is a plethora of information, much of which is not useful. However, through the CSM mass interview method the bureaucrat was able to identify the most important and useful information for transportation planners.

The following is an analysis of barriers to exchanging information and ways of over coming these restraints.

Barriers

1. No knowledge of what information is available or required by other offices or programs.
2. No formal process for the exchange of information between offices within DMT.
3. Lack of compatible hardware and software.
4. Turf.
5. Lack of participation or interest by a few people who may have a lot

of experience and knowledge.

6. Need for a clear format for gathering data; lack of common terminology may cause confusion.

7. People resist change.

8. Lack of timely information.

9. Lack of consistency in depth and level of detail and type of information; also, poor configuration of data files (project numbers, record type and record length).

10. Inadequate management support.

11. No knowledge of who to see and where.

Solutions to Barriers

1. Meet with each office to discuss the process the information center is going to use to collect information.

2. Develop a form to be used initially by each employee to give you ideas of what information they have and need.

3. Adopt and maintain a consistent, timely process in establishing information exchange between offices within DMT and TRC.

4. Ensure that users are properly trained and training materials are available.

5. Use friendly programs.

6. Adopt programs for both IBM and Macintosh.

7. Develop a working group to assist with the gathering of relevant information to be included in TRC.

8. Give continual feedback to staff on progress of TRC and what TRC is doing.

9. Market TRC as a turf neutral source of valuable information.

10. Provide an updated listing of who is responsible for maintaining and providing information.

11. Obtain buy-in from users.

12. Develop a formal procedure to share program information with TRC.

13. Have a service attitude.

14. Provide information via local area network so users can retrieve information whenever the need arises.

15. Establish a mechanism to verify information.

16. Provide clear, precise definition of information needed for TRC and efficient process.

17. Promote better communication within DMT.

18. Have a tour of the TRC when it is close to completion.

19. Designate an office resource person.

APPENDIX
STATEMENTS OF VISION, SERVICE, QUALITY
AND INFORMATION FOR THE TRANSIT RESOURCE CENTER

The slip analysis resulted in a vision statement, service concept, and quality definition. Included within the service concept, the participants identified major categories of transit information for the purpose of developing a transit resource data base.

The Vision

The Center is to be a broker of information. To provide a conduit of information exchange among the Division of Mass Transit, the twelve districts, transit operators, and regional operators.

The Center is to be adaptive to current trends and issues. The Center must adopt an open system philosophy managed by a continuous improvement concept; it should monitor and provide information regarding national and international trends in transit planning and technology.

The Center is to create networks to exchange information. This role includes identifying a list of peer to peer experts who can assist one another with very technical and complex transit related issues.

The Center is to be part of the information highway. Although reference materials such as manuals, videos, and reports will be maintained at the Center, the main thrust is to exchange information electronically.

The Service

Among the many ideas presented, the following list identifies those services that will be adopted.

1. Create an information center of reference and video material.
2. Establish a hot line for customers to seek information regarding such topics as grants, legislation, ADA, ISTEA, procurement, and other pertinent issues.
3. Provide a calendar of events for transit symposiums, forums, classes, etc.
4. Establish a network of peer to peer associations.
5. Provide information via LANs systems and modems.
6. Utilize the Electronic Bulletin Board to post information and receive requests.

The Quality

1. Allow customers to define quality through continuous feedback loops placed within the system.
2. Provide user friendly computer applications.
3. Provide credible and up to date information in a timely manner.

The Information

The 12 major categories consist of:

1. Calendar of events.
2. Transit statistical data.

3. Directory of agencies.
4. Peer to peer association.
5. Funding sources.
6. Transit related legislation.
7. Transit related research information.
8. Alternative fuel.
9. Vehicle and equipment procurement.
10. Transit connectivity.
11. Transit modes.
12. Planning references.

The above listed twelve major categories represented over 51 sub-categories including over 350 topics.

Chapter 13

Perspective on the CSM

The CSM has been used by managers, researchers, various types of analysts, consultants, writers, trainers and teachers. We have endeavored to display some of the variety of applications through a common framework applied in CSM cases. For each case we identified the importance of the study, background information which led to the intervention, the targets and how and why they were developed, organization of workshops, constraints on use of the method, findings and outcomes, and an appendix containing illustrative results of slip classification. Aspects of cases are recapitulated below under topical headings since the cases provide value added information on the CSM.

Importance of Cases

Under the topical heading, importance, each case explained why the CSM was used, considering the problem or objective and, more importantly, any adaptations or findings about CSM techniques. "The Century Freeway Project" case was a consulting application in which the major fact finding design had been developed through other research. The CSM was used for mass interviewing of information sources. "The County Personnel Department: Classification and Pay Division" case was a routine consulting intervention. However, its importance is that an effort was made to validate the CSM. This was demonstrated in a side-by-side display of CSM classified data and interview results based on different sample subjects from the same agency.

The importance of case titled "Survey of Training Needs and Training Program Development For a Community Redevelopment Agency" was in its use of the CSM in surveying training needs. One approach is demonstrated in this case. In the case: "Use of CSM in a Major State Agency to Surface Problems and Possible Solutions," the method was used to aid in the process of "reinventing government" for this agency. In the "Use of the CSM in Intervening in a Training Program for a Federal Agency" the method was used to deflect training participant resistance by allowing catharsis through slip writing and feedback of results. At the same time, valuable data on content and process of training were provided the trainer. It also provides an example of anonymously gathered data on slips.

The importance of the case titled "Survey of Experts on Earthquake Mitigation Management For Harbors and Sea Ports," is in demonstrating use of the CSM as a research tool. In this case the CSM was used with other methodologies in applied research on important technical and public policy issues. In "Writing Contracting Procedures For the Tactical Air Command" the importance lies in use of the technique to write procedures. The "Development of a Transit Resource Center" case illustrates the important use of the CSM in determining system requirements.

Background Information

Background provides information on the context of the study, including origin, entre and groups studied. "The Century Freeway Project" arose from litigation over the social consequences of construction of a California freeway. The lawsuit required various social actions such as providing employment opportunities for women and minorities, as well as utilizing women and minority contractors, and avoiding socially and economically disruptive effects of freeway construction. Several agencies were involved and many goals were not being achieved.

The seismic mitigation management study came about as a result of National Science Foundation funding of research on reducing the consequences of earthquakes in Pacific Basin seaports and harbors. A state bureaucrat charged with responsibility for "Development of a Transit Resource Center" had been previously trained in the CSM. Because of this training and the need for pooling ideas from many potential users, the CSM was the methodology of choice.

Target Development

Targeting logically follows background information—whether targets have to be opportunistically developed or if they can be based upon pre-understanding and, therefore, provide the basis for greater penetration of ideas. Targets in "The Century Freeway Project" case were predetermined by previous research. Most other cases involved "fishing expedition" targets (problems and solutions). Groups were asked to respond in "ing" language to targets in the "Use of CSM in a Major State Agency to Surface Problems and Possible Solutions." The case on "Survey of Training Needs and Training Program Development For a Community Redevelopment Agency" naturally used a target which queried project management personnel on perceived training needs to better perform their job. In the "Use of CSM in Intervening in a Training Program for a Federal Agency" participants were asked to respond to "troubles" targets in "How to" language, and in statements beginning with action verbs for recommendations to address problems.

In the case of "Writing Contracting Procedures for the Tactical Air Command" participants were instructed to write procedures for persons who would replace them on the job. Those procedures selected should be understood well by writers and be potentially problematic for successors. Targets resembled a combination of information system and strategic planning types of questions in the "Development of a Transit Resource Center" case.

Organization of Workshops and Constraints

Workshop organization may also result from opportunistic circumstances—Was data gathering part of another event, allowing only a "quickie" intervention? Could stake holder groups be segregated so as to aid in controlling the data collection? What about constraints? Were some questions not permitted; was the size or composition of the audience suboptimal?

The case on procedures writing for the Tactical Air Command is an example of an opportunistic intervention at a conference which was supposed to clarify contracting problems resulting from interpreting complex legal requirements, but which appeared destined to not achieve its objective. Because use of CSM was a fall back procedure, it was severely constrained by time limitations.

In the seismic mitigation management study the aggregation of experts was carried out by staging a conference. The conferees were willing to attend to hear and discuss papers presented by various specialists. The CSM intervention thus was possible only by enticing conference attendance of the experts of whom individual interviews would have been too costly and time consuming to carry out.

Data Classification, Findings and Outcomes

Data classification may lead to study outputs such as reports or publications. Sometimes outcomes or effects of interventions may be recognizable. The case: "Use of CSM in a Major State Agency to Surface

Problems and Possible Solutions" demonstrates how problems and solutions are integrated. The case: "Use of CSM in Intervening in a Training Program for a Federal Agency" is the only example presented in which slips were classified under a theoretical framework (organizations as social systems) rather than by inductively derived categories.

In the procedures writing case for the Tactical Air Command the output was a contracting manual composed of cookbook-like recipes for troublesome tasks.

Notes

[1] U. S. Department of Labor, Manpower Administration, *A Handbook for Job Restructuring*, 1970.

[2] Professor Ross Clayton was assisted in this study by Jerry Estensen, Peter Roddy, and Peggy Volstedt.

[3] Gilbert B. Siegel and Dorothy M. Bjur, "Earthquake Mitigation Management for Harbors and Seaports." Based on work supported by the National Science Foundation Grant No. CEE 83-14227. Los Angeles: School of Public Administration and Institute of Marine and Coastal Studies, University of Southern California, August, 1985: 189-196.

[4] Gilbert B. Siegel, "The State of Seismic Mitigation Management in U. S. Pacific Basin Seaports and Harbors," *International Journal of Mass Emergencies and Disasters*, 7, N. 2 (August 1989): 168-182; "What a Major Earthquake Would Do to Our Harbors," *Long Beach Press Telegram*, October 11, 1985.

[5] This case was developed by Beverly K. Brazeau, Associate Transportation Planner, State of California, Department of Transportation.

Crawford Slip Method Bibliography

Air Force Logistics Management Center. "Copper '90: A Plan for Air Force Base-Level Contracting for the 1990's." AFLMC Project LC830105, Lt. Col. C. Richard Porth, Project Manager, December 1984.

Crawford, C. C. 'How to Study by the Crawford Slip Method." Unpublished paper, undated.

Crawford, C. C. "How You Can Gather and Organize Ideas Quickly." *Chemical Engineering* July 25 1983: 87-90.

Crawford, C. C. "Crawford Slip Method (CSM)." *Air Force Journal of Logistics* Spring 1985: 28-30.

Crawford, C. C. Professor Teaches 'How to' Study." *Educator.* Air Force Institute of Technology, WPAFB, OH 45433, May 1985: 4-5.

Crawford, C. C., et. al. "Complexity Crisis." *Logistics Spectrum* Summer 1984: 7-12.

Crawford, C. C. and J. W. Demidovich. "Program Management Suggestions: How to Manage Development and Acquisition of Weapon Systems." Fort Belvoir, VA: Defense System, Management College, October 29 1979.

Crawford, C. C. and J. W. Demidovich. "Think Tank Technology for Systems Management." *Journal of Systems Management* November 1981: 22-5.

Crawford, C. C. and J. W. Demidovich. *Crawford Slip Method: How to Mobilize Brainpower by Think Tank Methodology.* Los Angeles, CA: School of Public Administration, University of Southern California, 1983.

Crawford, C. C. and J. W. Demidovich. "Looking for Leaks and Losses: How to Reduce Logistics Costs by the Crawford Slip Method." *Logistics Spectrum* Fall 1983: 20-4.

Crawford, C. C., J. W. Demidovich, and R. M. Krone. "Instructing and Commentary, How to Recycle and Improve by the Crawford Slip Method." Unpublished paper, undated.

Crawford, C. C., J. W. Demidovich, and Robert M. Krone. *Productivity by the Crawford Slip Method: How to Write, Publish, Instruct, Supervise, and Manage for Better Job Performance.* Los Angeles, CA: School of Public Administration, University of Southern California, 1984.

Crawford, C. C. and R. M. Krone. "Supplier Partnership in the Aerospace and Defense Industries." Houston, TX: Coopers and Lybrand, 1990.

Crawford, C. C. and G. B. Siegel. "Developing Imbedded or On-the-Job Training Methods." Proposal to the Office of Naval Research, April 1986.

Crawford, C. C., G. B. Siegel, and J. W. Demidovich. "Productive Money Management: How to Improve the Work of Military Comptrollers." *Armed Forces Comptroller* Fall 1985: 4-7.

Crawford, C. C., G. B. Siegel, and J. A. Kerr. "Learning Needs of Contracting Personnel, Feedback from 62 Contracting Educators in a Crawford Slip Method Workshop." *National Contract Management Journal* 23 (2 1990): 55-66.

Clayton, R. and C. C. Crawford. *Authorship for Productivity by the Crawford Slip Method (CSM).* Los Angeles, CA: School of Public Administration, University of Southern California, undated.

Demidovich, J. W. and C. C. Crawford. "Why Be an Air Force Engineer?" *Air Force Engineering and Service Quarterly* Fall 1982: 34-5.

Demidovich, J. W. and C. C. Crawford. "Linkages and Logistics: How to Improve Coordination by The Crawford Slip Method." *Logistics Spectrum* Winter 1983.

Fiero, J. "Implementing Total Quality Improvement, Identifying Problems Using the Crawford Slip Method." Scottsdale, AZ: Improving Engineering Effectiveness, Inc., undated.

Goldstein, C. M., A. B. Rosenblum, and C. C. Crawford. "Dental Productivity." *Journal of Dental Practice and Administration* July/September 1986: 111-16.

Hanson, Lars P. "Automating the Crawford Slip Method." Unpublished research paper. University of Southern California, December 19 1986.

Illif, R. "An Outline for the Development of Computer Software to Support the Crawford Slip Method." Unpublished paper written for the University of Southern California graduate course in "Systems Management and Organization Theory." November-December 1984.

Knez, R. "Sharing Human Intelligence Through a Computer Network." *Defense Management Journal* First Quarter 1983: 43-4.

Knouse, S. B. *Crawford Slip Method: How to Mobilize Brainpower by Think Tank Technology* by C. C. Crawford and J. W. Demidovich, a review, *Personnel Psychology* 36 (Winter 1983): 1014-15.

Krone, R. M. "A Systems Improvement Method for Managers." *Systems Science and Science* Proceedings of the 26th Annual Meeting of the Society for General Systems Research, Washington, D. C., January 5-9, 1982: 847-60.

Krone, R. M. "A Pacific Nuclear Information Group: Prospects and Guidelines." *Journal of East Asian Affairs* 3 (Fall/Winter 1983): 422-44.

Krone, R. M. "Problem Formulation Through Networking with the Crawford Slip Method." *Systems Inquiring: Theory, Philosophy, Methodology*. Proceedings of the Society for General Systems Research , International Conference, Los Angeles, May 27-31, 1985, Bela H. Banathy, Editor-in-Chief, Vol 1" 482-7.

Krone, R. M. "Brainpower Networking for Systems Managers: Sabbatical Research Report, Executive Summary." University of Southern California, February 24, 1986.

Krone, R. M. "The St. Louis Arch and Union Station: How to Merge Artificial Intelligence with the Crawford Slip Method." Unpublished workshop report to Professor Joel Isaacson of the Computer Science Department, Southern Illinois University, Edwardsville, June 10 1986.

Krone, R. M. "Management of Operational Knowledge through Brainpower Networking and the Crawford Slip Method." *Proceedings* of the IEEE National Conference on Management and Technology, Atlanta, October 27-30, 1987.

Krone, R. M. "Translating Systems Theory to Systems Improvement." Paper presented at the 1987 meting of the Far West Region, International Society for General Systems Research, Sacramento, CA, August 30, 1987.

Krone, R. M. "Brainpower Dynamics in High Technology Projects." A chapter in *Handbook of Technology Management: Modern Practices in Engineering, Science and Research*, Dundar F. Kocaoglu, Ed. John Wiley & Sons, 1988.

Krone, R. M. and C. C. Crawford. "Total National Security: Mobilizing Brainpower." *The Bureaucrat* 14 (April 1985): 36-40.

Krone, R. M. and C. H. Clark. "Brainpower Productivity."Unpublished paper, October 1988.

Krone, R. M., J. W. Demidovich, and C. C. Crawford. "A Computer on Every Desk?" *The Bureaucrat* 13 (Winter 1984-85): 58-63.

Mitchell, C. R. "Microcomputer Implementation of Crawford Slip Method." Unpublished paper written for the University of Southern California graduate course in "Systems Management and O r g a n i z a t i o n Theory," January-March 1984.

Rusk, R. A. and R. M. Krone "The Crawford Slip Method (CSM) as a Tool for Extraction of Expert Knowledge." *Human-Computer Interaction*, G. Salvendy, Ed. Amsterdam: Elsever Science Publishers, 1984: 279-82.

Rusk, R. A. and R. M. Krone. "The Crawford Slip Method and Performance Improvement." *Human Factors in Organizational Design and Management*, H. W. Hedrick and O. Brown, Eds. North-Holland: Elsevier Science Publishers, 1984: 251-57.

Siegel, G. B. and C. C. Crawford. "Analyzing Roles of Productivity Improvement Managers: A Crawford Slip Method Case Example." *Management Science and Policy Analysis* Summer 1987.

Siegel, G. B. "Port of L. A., Industrial and Administration Audit, Human Resources." R. J. A. Management Services and Booze Allen, and Hamilton, May/June 1987.

Siegel, G. B. "County of Riverside, Personnel Department, Organizational Design." R. J. A. Management Services, January 1987.

Siegel, G. B. "Century Freeway Management Study." R. J. A. Management Services and Price Waterhouse, September 1988.

Siegel, G. B. "Selection of Pasadena City Manager." R. J. A. Management Services and Shannon Associates, August 1989.

Siegel, G. B. "L. A. Community Redevelopment Agency, Survey of Training Needs and Program Development," April 1989-May 1990.

Siegel, G. B. "Crawford Slip Method, Assessment of Training Needs for Labor Relations/Management Supervisory Skills." American P r e s i - dent Companies, October 1990.

Stoddard, J. B. "Expert Systems, Lessons of the Crawford Slip Method." Stoddard Productivity Systems, Inc., undated.

Thorsness, L. K. "Teen-Age Leadership: Youth Help Youth to Take Responsibility." *North Dakota Farm Bureau* April 1984.

Zachary, W. B. and R. M. Krone. "Managing Creative Individuals in High Technology Research Projects." *IEEE Transactions in Engineering Management*, Special Issue on Managing Technical Professionals, February 1984.

Originally prepared by Robert M. Krone and supplemented by Gilbert B. Siegel

Index